INTRODUCTION

In my years I have helped dozens of start-up coffee shops achieve their goal. Some people believe that they can go into a business without planning. They think that they do not need help when it comes to strategizing, pricing and choosing a location. To these people I have one thing to say: You are wrong. I have seen many businesses rise and fall within a span of months, and I have seen many rise to the top and stay there consistently, month after month, year after year. The common pattern found in failing businesses is that they do not accept the help of people who have tried and failed themselves. Of course I have had numerous failures over the years, which is why I am the perfect person to help you start your business from the ground up and turn it into a success. I have learned from my failures and it is my job to help you avoid going down that path. I know what to do because I know what *not* to do. Dozens of coffee shops have seen the light of day because of my help.

This book was created to help yours do the same. It is my sole purpose to add your name to the list of people whose lives and business I have had the pleasure of impacting and growing in the past.

LOCATION SELECTION SECRETS

The first thing you want to do when starting a coffee shop is to find the perfect location. Chances are that you already have a business idea in mind. You have a certain look and clientele in mind. Now you need to find the best location to suit your business. It's time for you to translate those dreams and plans to reality and choosing the best location is a great place to start. Once you have that, you can plan the rest of the business. How much will you need to earn to cover rent? How will you decorate your space and how much will that cost? Here are a few things to keep in mind, as well as a few tips to help you make your decision.

Stand vs café

One of the biggest decisions to make is whether you want a stand or a café. There are pros and cons for both these options. Both are perfect for their intended purpose so let's assess each of them—their uses and all the aspects you'll need to take into account when considering either option.

Stand

The first thing we will examine is a coffee stand. Certainly the cheaper option of the two, coffee stands are great for serving the on-the-go customers who don't have the time to sit down and drink their beverage at a leisurely pace. Coffee stands are most commonly found in major cities or rural areas where the customer can get their order and be on their way. This being said, location is important. Do you intend on opening a coffee shop in Eureka Springs or New York? Stands are only useful for major cities such as New York and won't be a good idea in smaller towns. As smaller towns aren't as corporate as major cities, people aren't in a rush unlike most commuters and people who are always on the go within the hustle and bustle of big metropolitan cities such as New York or Seattle.

Another great thing about a coffee stand is that people tend to avoid the 'guilt' after treating them-selves to a cup of coffee. When sitting down at a café, it's easy to feel unproductive or even overindulge in more pastries and other sweet treats. However, at a coffee stand, the price of your coffee will be a fraction of the price you'd pay at a café. People tend to feel less guilty when buying their daily dose of coffee from a coffee or food stand as opposed to how they might feel when eating or drinking at a coffee shop. They don't waste any time, they pay a lot less and they get to enjoy good coffee even when they are on-the-go.

Stands can be just as profitable as a café considering the low overhead costs. You won't need the same number of employees as a café might and the sheer amount of people you can serve in a single day far outweighs the number of customers that visit coffee shops.

That being said, coffee stands have to provide affordable consumables which means the profit you will make in a day might be equal to or less than a coffee shop because you can get away with charging much more in a café. The flow of business is also almost constant which means long, gruesome hours.

Café

With the right game plan and strategies, it should be relatively easy to start a café. They are great for business people and although a coffee stand is good for corporate locations, there is the problem of limited to no seating space. A café, although it has a lofty overhead, is perfect for hosting large crowds and creating a comfortable and charming space.

Coffee is definitely one of the most loved beverages in the world. Generally speaking, having a place where people can come together, mix, mingle, and connect with each others while they can enjoy a beverage is the perfect combination. A coffee shop has the sort of intimacy that makes people want to go back to it day after day, week after week. When you have a coffee shop, it gives you an opportunity to create a charming atmosphere that will definitely make it a local favorite. Compared to a coffee stand, a café has more potential to build a regular clientele. Coffee stands come and go and people don't really care when a stand moves to another spot or gets replaced, most don't even notice, but when a café changes, people get upset. They notice, and they mourn the loss of a familiar place. There's a reason for that. They get attached, they find comfort, they find joy, and they find community and culture, which is exactly what you want to cultivate when you open a café. Despite the massive overhead and extra staff, a café is definitely worth it. The question is: Which one would you prefer? A speedy, on-the-go stand or a comfortable café with loyal clientele?

How to look for a shop

Honestly, you can have the best cappuccino in the state, but how will people know about it or buy it if you do not have the right location for it? The success of your coffee stand or café hinges on location, primarily at least. It's easy to get caught up in decorating, curating a menu, creating the ideal ambience, and forgetting all about the location. However, the location is no small detail and should on the top of your priority list.

Getting the cheapest building might seem

appealing at first, but there's a reason why it's so cheap. It's either falling apart or in an irrelevant location. Most commonly, it's the latter. Rather, spend a little bit more and rent a proper location rather than a cheap place where no one will even find you. Consider every possible option before deciding on a building or location for your stand or café. If you are a local, chances are that you already know where the hotspots are. That is where you want your shop to be located. If you are new to town, you might want to consider hiring a professional to help you find a place.

Things to factor

Here are some things to consider when choosing a location

- Demographics

Consider the demographics of the area. What is the traffic like? How many people will pass your shop on the daily? You want as many people to pass your shop as possible but don't be unrealistic. Consider the population and do the math.

- Terms of the lease

Now, there are two ways this can go. You can either sign a long-term lease that will lock your rent and guarantee the location of your shop for a good amount of time. The problem with this is that, if your business does not succeed, you will be stuck with paying for the lease. On the flip side, let's say that you sign a short lease and you are successful, what happens when that lease is up and your landlord does not want to renew it? You'll have to pack up your café and move elsewhere, leaving the beautiful community and environment you have cultivated at your café in a lurch. Remember that retail leases are complex and people often try to scam new tenants. Have an attorney look over your lease before you sign anything. Negotiate and come to terms that suit you both.

- Neighbors

Just like buying a house, knowing what the neighbors are like is important. Why? Because they might scare off your customers. If you are located next to a strip club, chances are that you will not get the sort of clientele you are aiming for. If it's next to an apartment building, are they loud or not? Will they cause trouble? It's important to know what sort of businesses surround you and if it's domestic housing, you'll have to be sure that it is suitable for your business.

- Where are the customers at?

Make sure you know where the customers are and where their usual 'spots' are. You can't open a toy store surrounded by old-age-homes, so don't start a coffee shop in a similarly dead-end location. Make sure that you study the demographic properly to determine where the target clientele dwells. What route do they take to work?

• Safety

One of the most important things to consider is safety. When a person goes to a store, they want to know that they won't get robbed as soon as they exit. When people visit a coffee shop, they want to know that they are safe to sit down and enjoy their beverages without having to look over their shoulders the entire time. Another reason why safety is important is your shop itself. You want to know that you are not an easy target to get robbed. All that hard work only to get robbed at the end of the day? No. Safety is a priority and should be at the very top of your list. Do the right amount of research about crime in the area and act accordingly when selecting a location.

• Zoning restrictions

Without knowing it, you might restrict yourself to some strict zoning restrictions. Some areas limit the times at which you can operate which means the times you can open your coffee shop is restricted. Most zoning restrictions are reasonable, but if you intend on opening a late-night coffee house, make sure the zoning restrictions allow you to. Some zoning restrictions also control the type of signage you can put up and the type of business you are allowed to conduct.

- Look for a potential competitor and use it to your advantage

Chances are that you already have competitors in the area. Use that to your advantage. How? Well, your competitors already took the time and money to do the marketing. Why not use that? They have put up signs to attract people's attention and that is where you come in. Try finding a location close to your competitor. Use their marketing to attract customers. It only takes one customer to enjoy your coffee and atmosphere more. The rest will soon follow to test this theory. If you are hidden out of sight, people won't know about your store. You want as much exposure as possible. If this is the route you are taking, make sure that you can compete with them successfully.

- The size of the facility

It doesn't help to have a good-looking facility that isn't big enough to host the sort of crowd you wish to attract. Small spaces can be attractive in more ways than one, but customers do not want to feel claustrophobic when sitting in your café or while waiting for coffee at the counter. Size is important.

- Layout

Keep your layout requirements in mind when you are choosing a space. Sure, some spaces might be nice to look out with a lot of potential, but does it have potential for your needs? Always keep your business and ideas in mind when choosing. It's easy to get overwhelmed.

- Repairs

If the building you are possibly moving into needs repairs, chances are that it will need a lot of it and honestly, it's not worth it. Not only will it delay your launch date, but it will also cost money that you didn't intend on spending. It's a hassle and no matter how 'fun' the estate agent might make this DIY project seem, it might just be the reason why the previous tenants moved out. Some repairs are impossible to make without a big budget and it has to be safe for your customers as well. Make sure plumbing and electrical wires are up to standard. Keep away from places where you have to rewire or replace plumbing. Also, make sure that there is adequate ventilation.

- Accessibility

How close to your shop do your target customers live? Is it easily accessible? How about employees? Will you be able to find and train competent people for your coffee shop? Not many people take this into consideration, but it plays an important role when opening any business. It has to be easily accessible by both employees and customers. Not to mention having deliveries made.

How to get a good deal

There are a number of marketing ideas that will make your efforts that much easier. This isn't the 1970's anymore where marketing was restricted to newspaper articles and television. Nowadays there is a good number of platforms where you can expand your reach. Social media is your friend in more ways than one. Here is a list of platforms where you have the potential to find good deals and then some. Don't go for the first, best thing that pops up. There is always a better deal out there if only you looked.

- Facebook, Instagram, Twitter, etc.

Any social media platform is your friend. The marketplace on Facebook is a great way to find real estate and any other things you might need for your coffee shop. This will also lead to notifications being sent to you whenever something new goes on sale that you might be interested in and that is the best thing that could happen. Deals come when it's least expected and getting notifications about them will no doubt help you secure a good one. Don't be afraid of browsing social media offers for real estate. It is cost effective and makes life much easier. The only warning I can give you is to make sure everything is legitimate. Do some research and look at the facility yourself. Don't believe the pictures.

- Craigslist

Over the years, Craigslist has gained a poor reputation thanks to scammers but the truth is that scammers exist anywhere you look. People just aren't educated enough to know when they are being scammed and believe that any random person on the internet is an honest human being. Just like social media, do your homework before you commit to anything.

- Newspaper ads

This might be a little old-school, but it is definitely still relevant. Keep an eye on your newspaper's real estate offers. A lot of people might be ignoring these pages completely. Who even reads the newspaper anymore anyway? This can lead to good deals that your competitor might not have even seen yet.

- Town Hall

An old-school way of doing it, but snooping around your town hall is a great way to spot any deals. There will be a variety of eviction notices and probationary listing available as well as an array of other information. You want to be the first to know when a tenant is being evicted and the best way to do that is by keeping an eye out for eviction notices. Those landlords are desperate for new tenants which means their price will be low. They can't afford the facility to be empty for too long which means they will do whatever is necessary to get a new tenant moved in as soon as possible. This is great for negotiation and trust me, there is always room for that.

- A variety of real estate agents and their websites

Don't limit yourself to one real estate agent. Instead, browse the other agents' websites and what they have on offer. Chances are that there will be a wide variety of options for you to choose from when you take this extra step. If you have other options, people tend to go above and beyond to give you a good deal. Browse as much as you can and look at as many facilities as possible. Consider every deal and go with what the best one is. Take everything into consideration from what is included in the rent to where the facility is located. Do your homework so you can't be talked into something you know nothing about. Most real estate agents rely on you not having any knowledge about the buildings or neighborhood and will talk you into anything to make a quick sale. Negotiate and know what the place is worth.

What price range should be looking at

There is one main thing that decides the price of the facility that you are looking at and that is location, location, location. In what town or city is your venue located? Is it in a mall or a stand-alone store? Sunnyside, cityscape or sea-view? What is the foot traffic like? All of this makes a difference.

It's also all about supply in demand. If there is limited space for rent, landlords will charge more for their space because they don't have other landlords to compete with. Do your research and make sure that the facility is really as rare as the landlord claims it is. Also, make sure that you get all of the positives that push the price up so much. Keep in mind that you might get away with cheaper if you are looking for a nice and cozy, tucked away coffee shop that relies on advertising and word of mouth to get customers. Just remember that you might have to spend the money you save on rent on advertising your business. You might even lose money because of the location.

Also, remember that prize isn't everything. If you are paying top dollar per square feet, you have to be sure that you will be getting customers. Don't let the price mislead you as going for the more expensive option is not always the best route to go. Getting the best deal for your specific needs will take a lot of research in the town or city you will be establishing your shop. Manhattan is going to be more expensive than Staten Island. That is a given. No matter where you are, Manhattan will be more expensive so take the town or city into consideration. Price ranges change in every town so be sure to know the market value of real estate in the area.

PRODUCT SELECTION SECRETS

*W*hat to sell

Determining what to sell starts with determining the customer's needs. Every successful business caters to the needs of the public. Here are some tips to uncover what the people need.

- Study existing data

As I have mentioned before, if you are reading this book, you are not new to the coffee shop business. Chances are that you already know what customers want and what is lacking in the marketplace. Take a closer look at what you have learned over the years and contemplate how you can improve or match what your employers did that was popular with the public. If the people enjoyed decaf, perhaps expand your menu and experiment with different blends. If tea is being sought after by the clientele, add different kinds of tea to the menu. You have a wealth of knowledge inside your mind. Don't be afraid to use it to your advantage. You know how things work, you know what the people want and need. It also won't hurt to read up on it a little. Do research on popular beverages and meals in the area? What are the locals like and what do they want?

- Interview people

Sometimes talking to people is the most frightening part of the entire process but if you have worked with people in a coffee shop before, you know exactly what to say to butter their buns. Ask them what they need and what they would like to see in a coffee shop. What are the other coffee shops lacking that you can add to yours? What does the public want to see that can make your coffee stand or café stand out above all the other coffee shops in the area? Ask random people on the streets, you might even want to set up a table and chair somewhere to allow people to write down their complaints and concerns about the local coffee shops. All of this will help shape an idea of what you should sell. No town is the same and everyone has different tastes. You can't use your knowledge that you learned in California to open a coffee shop in Arizona. The best way to learn what the town or city wants is to interview their locals and find out what they want and need. What are they short on and what do they have an abundance of? Your goal is to create something unique that people would love to come back to.

- Analyze your competition

If there is a coffee shop around that has been around for years and years, they must be doing something right. If there is a Starbucks that is constantly jam-packed and making a killing, they have found the secret to pleasing the public. Study this and try to figure out how exactly you are going to incorporate that into your own business. The goal is not to match then, but to climb to the top with new and fresh ideas built on the foundations of what the people want. So they want affordable baked goods and coffee? Use that and come up with a combo. Two in one. They don't have to order separately and it's a little cheaper than buying both. It doesn't take a genius to come up with ideas that will attract the public's attention. All you need is a little research. Combine everything you have learned from different competitors and create an offer where they get everything in one spot. The comfort, the good coffee, and donuts for an affordable price.

It won't be long until you can't keep up with customers.

- Keep record of experiences

Make sure to ask people about their experiences at other coffee shops. Ask them what they don't like. How is the customer service? Do they prefer friendly banter or a business-as-usual attitude? How are they experiencing the products they are getting from your competitors? Are they enjoying it? What would they change? What was the general experience? Record all of these answers and be sure to keep all of the positive things the same and work on the negatives. Use your competition's mistakes to your advantage.

- Study complaints and praises

This counts for both before and after you open your shop. Listen to the complaints and praises of other shops before and listen to your own when your shop is open. Don't get offended when a person doesn't like a certain thing on your menu. Some locals might not be used to the strong coffee you are used to serving. Merely adapt the menu accordingly. It's a learning process and the sooner you realize that listening to your customers will help you, the faster you will get your shop perfect in the eyes of the public. What you like might not be what they do and vice versa. Be open to complaints and praises. Be open to feedback, it's a gift! You are not going to make money by serving yourself, you have to serve others.

How to price

- Inspect the market

It's no use deciding on the price of your items if your customers won't be willing to pay. It's also important to know how much your competitors charge and try to match or go below that. When a new place opens up, chances are that your competitors will try to beat your price in an attempt to retain their customers. It's all just business so don't be afraid to challenge them. There are some people who are willing to pay more for better quality, but some prefer the cheaper option. Make sure you know which client type you will be catering too.

- Work out your costs

That being said, you can't go too low, though. You have to work out the costs of your company and work from there. Include all the money you will have to spend. That includes the development of your products, the staff, rent, and everything in between. Make sure you will not be suffering a loss and are actually earning a profit. Being the cheapest coffee shop around is not worth losing money over. Rather keep your prices reasonable, somewhere in the middle, so both you and your clients win.

- Pricing techniques

There are two very effective pricing techniques. The one involves determining the value your clientele will attach to your product. This means that, if you have high-quality beverages and perhaps some light lunches, you have to determine how important your customers will find what you offer in a day to day life. The next option is pretty simple too. All you have to do is add a mark-up percentage to the cost of the product. Keep in mind that you should also take the time preparing the product into consideration. Time is money, after all. Personally I have found that the cost-plus pricing works the best and by far the simplest.

- Consider all factors

How will VAT impact the prices? Keep that in mind when you are coming up with costs for your products. Including VAT might have a very high impact on the price depending on what you charge for the products. Keep margins modest in order to get more sales and keep your prices as low as possible to compete with other coffee shops. If you intend on having fewer and wealthier customers, this must also be taken into consideration but it is not as important as it is when you are trying to keep the costs as low as possible.

- Keep up to date with the market

Things change overnight and so does the market. Prices aren't always fixed and sometimes you might order the same amount of coffee beans as you usually do, but don't only focus on pricing at the end of the day. This will cause you to lose money instead. It also helps to talk to customers to ensure the prices are to their satisfaction. Everything on the market changes and when prices of ingredients go up, so should your prices for your products. Just keep in mind that people are not fond of change so make sure that you do it subtly and keep the price in the same category as the customer you are serving.

What is better to sell at the beginning, what to sell later down the line

It is best to start out simple and go from there. I often see people who want to go all out from the very start, but I will always advise against it. You have to crawl before you can walk, and you have to walk before you can run. This is the best way you can think about this. Start with ten beverages if you are running a café. Don't start with fifty different flavors of coffee. Try things out first and get rid of the things that don't sit well with your customers. You have to experiment to find the perfect mix.

Do what you know first and play it safe. Add something every month until you have the menu you have always dreamed about. There are set beverages that people love and if you are going to start with things they may not like, that might lose you some customers.

How To Hire, and find the right people: Experienced vs. Inexperienced

The age long debate is on whether or not you should hire someone with experience or someone with no experience at all. My advice would be to hire a well balanced crew going. What do I mean by that? Well, having experience is good and all, but that experience comes with a price. Instead of hiring two experienced waiters, hire one with experience and one without. That way, the more experienced waiter can help you train the newbie without any prior experience and it saves you money. Not only does this create job opportunities for young people, but it's also a great way to show the community that you are supporting them too. By hiring their youth, you are giving them a chance and that is how you will earn the support of the community. Hire enough people with experience, but create an opportunity where people can constantly learn new things and gain experience. The problem with many places is that they want people with experience, however if they aren't willing to hire people without any prior experience, those people will never get the opportunity to gain any experience. A community is easy to win over when you are shaping a future for their kids.

This being said, don't tip the scales and hire too many inexperienced staff members. Experienced should outweigh un-experienced. That way there are more people to teach the newbie a lot of different things and your café will have a professional feel as there are people working there who actually know what they are doing.

Hiring and Interviews

Hiring the wrong employee is an expensive mistake and you might end up in much bigger debt before you get the money flowing. Hiring the right employee can make the biggest difference in any business, not only a coffee shop. Your goal is to build a good relationship with your employees and you will automatically do that if they are good workers. This will create a positive working environment and have an enormous impact on the atmosphere of the coffee shop.

- Do a job analysis

What exactly do you need this employee to do? Doing a job analysis will allow you to take a better look at the job and what you need from it. What are the duties and necessary skills to do this particular job? You have to develop a good and detailed job description if you want to find the perfect employees for your business and to do that you need to do an analysis. Do you see how it all fits together perfectly?

- Work with a strategy

When conducting interviews, make future plans in your head. How well will they be able to train other employees in the future and are they coachable? Are they willing to learn? These are things that you can easily see while conducting the interview. Think about long-term instead of the opening month. Many people only want to hire people to help them out during the business launch and opening and continuously hire new staff every month or two. That isn't the sort of environment you want to create. If it's secure, your staff will feel comfortable which makes their interactions with customers so much better. It's all a cycle and you have to take everything into consideration.

- Ask the important questions

There are few things as intimidating as going for an interview and to be honest, if it is your first time as an interviewer, it can be just as scary. The first time I conducted an interview, I had to wear my blaze jacket the entire time because I was sweating through my shirt. It wasn't a formal interview at all and the heat was killing us all, but I had to choose between looking like a professional and looking as if I just stepped out of the gym. Now, the key that I have learned to conducting interviews is to ask the right questions. Don't dance around the topic and don't come at it with an angle. Make a list of questions you want to ask. Questions will change with every position you are trying to fill and doing research on the topics can help you immensely. Being prepared will set your mind at ease while making sure you ask the important questions that will make sure you get a good a good employee.

- Credentials

When setting out to hire experienced employees, it is important to review their credentials. It's easy to lie on a resume. Take it from a professional. If I did everything I did what I said I could do on my resume, I should have been a genius that was a hundred years old because it's impossible to do all of those things in the amount of time I have been working. Make sure your prospective employee's credentials check out. If it looks too good to be true, that's probably because it is. Check backgrounds and references. Many people list references, thinking that employers will never really check up on them. That is exactly why you should contact their references and make sure the new employee is really as good as they claim they are.

• Checklist

I love a checklist. Personally, I think it's one of the things I love most about an interview. I have the sort of mind that thinks about a hundred different things at once. And as good as it to have an active mind, things tend to get mixed up and crazy very quickly. There are just certain things that you need to do to stay on track and a checklist is the best way to do just that.

A checklist will systematize the hiring process and keep everything on track. This sets you at ease during interviews and it gives the potential employee an idea of what exactly you are looking for in your staff members. It's just overall a great thing to have and being organized is necessary if you plan on making a success of your business.

EQUIPMENT SELECTION SECRETS

So, you have your location, the promise of good employees, and a plan of action. The next step is getting the equipment you need.

Now, as someone who has some experience in coffee shops, chances are that you know the equipment inside out. But there are things that you might be missing and not taking into consideration, so here is a quick rundown on equipment you will need to open your coffee shop.

Equipment to Get

- Fridges and displays

With coffee comes milk… If you don't intend on selling food, you'll still have products to keep fresh. In the case that you are going to sell food, you'll need display fridges as well as fridges behind the counters. People want to see what they are buying and who can resist a slice of that delicious looking cheesecake in the display? In addition, you also want a display to keep hot foods, well, hot. Microwaving is not an option which means you need to keep the food warm as long as possible.

- Automatic drip coffee makers

Personally, I am not a black coffee sort of guy but statistics don't lie. Black coffee will be about 30% of your coffee shop's sales, so getting a high quality drip coffee maker has to be at the very top of the list. These are things that you can't save money on. They have to be high quality and durable. Remember that you want to make high quantities of coffee in a day and your equipment has to be durable and efficient. It's a smart idea to have multiple coffee makers as chances are that you will have times where the coffee shop is buzzing and you won't be able to keep up while serving customers.

- Coffee grinder

There's nothing like the smell of fresh coffee beans to create an ambience in a coffee shop. It's probably one of the only reasons people visit a coffee shop instead of having coffee at home. Customers like knowing that the coffee is freshly ground and there's just something about the sound that makes a coffee shop feel authentic. Now, obviously you can't use a food blender for this task. You have to get a high quality coffee grinder to keep up with the quantities you have to grind every day. Buying a once-off high quality coffee grinder will save you money in the future.

- An espresso machine

There is no chance that you will be able to get away cheap with an Espresso machine. There just isn't a chance of that happening. Espresso machines that are the quality you are looking for can cost you a small fortune but the fact is that there is always some element of espresso that is incorporated into other coffee blends. It is something that you cannot cut corners with, so don't even attempt it. It will leave you with a terrible machine and will cost you more in the long run.

- Devices Used for Cooking

Most coffee shops sell light lunches and baked goods along with their coffees and it's a smart idea to do all of this yourself. Yes, get a chef and make those sandwiches in-house. Bake those muffins and make those tarts. This means getting ovens, toasters, and other devices you need to produce the food you want to serve in your coffee shop.

- Shelves

Something that people tend to overlook is shelving. I once worked in a coffee shop that sold more products than actual coffee. They had shelves lining the walls from top to bottom and held a wealth of coffees, mugs, accessories and French presses. It annoyed me to no end to see how many of those things actually sold. I signed up to be a barista, not a retail store clerk. It was maddening. But the facts stay that those things work. And in order for you to sell things successfully, you need shelves to showcase them. Selling things in addition to the coffee shop can either be a hit or miss and that is solely because of shelving. If you don't have proper shelving, chances are that your coffee shop will seem crowded and cluttered. This makes it an unpleasant environment.

- Containers, Pumps, and Assorted Miscellaneous

My mother used to say that going to the container store was the top point of her days out. She used to walk around in there, not buying anything. As a child, I thought that she was a complete and utter freak, but as a grown up, I can see the appeal. There's just something about having things neatly tucked away in containers that is oddly satisfying.

In relation to this, this means that you need pumps, containers, boxes and disposable cups if you intend on allowing takeaway coffees.

Trust me, this is not something you want to cut corners with. Without suitable storage for the beans, syrups, and everything else you need for the intended menu, the shop will look cluttered and unorganized. It will exude a cluttered, unorganized, and unwelcoming vibe, driving everyone mad soon enough.

- POS System

Another thing people tend to overlook is a POS system. You need your inventory set up and your sales managed. You cannot do any of that without a reliable POS system. I will suggest cloud-based POS systems but that is persona taste only. I like things that are as easy and user friendly as humanly possible. I am also a control freak so this means that I will be able to keep track of every-thing all the time. Do some research and decide what kind of system would suit your needs best. You might not need overly fancy software, or you might be the sort of person who enjoys complicated which means there are more advanced options for you.

Decorating and Layout

Have you seen those coffee shop designing games they advertise on Facebook with every video you watch? The only problem with those is that there are only options for the color schemes and you can't move the actual furniture around. It sucks. But this is the perfect opportunity to live out your dreams. They layout and design can be a tricky business, but it is probably the most fun part of starting the business. You want to keep your own style, to incorporate it into the coffee shop itself while still keeping it as practical and 'clean' as possible. Here are some tips to help you achieve that.

- Create a clear concept

Sometimes it's just good to sit down and get a clear picture of what you want to do with the space and how you are going to do it. The key is to make it appealing for your customers and not for you alone while keeping a part of your personality as well. You want your coffee shop to be unique but still be appealing. This is the first step to designing and deciding on the design of your coffee shop. The design will also depend on the sort of people you want to attract. Will it be modern, old-school, rocker, punk, book-inspired, hipster? This is the step where you get to decide and work out what you want to do with the space. You need a clear idea before you can even begin furnishing the place. It might be a good idea to draw up a rough layout of your shop and figure out where you want to place everything. If it's a smaller space, I'd say this step is a must to make sure everything fits.

- Utilize the space.
- Smaller coffee shops have a certain sort of charm to them. It is instantly more appealing because it looks cozy and gives the illusion that there will be fewer queues and less waiting time on orders. Another good thing about smaller spaces is that there are fewer seating options which means fewer distractions and more work being done.

A small space might be cozy and will lure those customers in, but there is one small problem (see what I did there? No? Okay, moving on!).

With a small building comes limited space. That means that everything has to be placed strategically so the space doesn't look crowded and cluttered. Make use of walls and hang shelves. Space the tables and chairs smartly to avoid your staff walking into them. Personally, I hate weaving my way through small, crowded spaces so a coffee shop with room to walk and sit peacefully with few people around to bother me is perfect.

- Electronics

Wifi is a must nowadays and there is no two ways about it. I was in South Africa a few months ago and I found that people preferred going to coffee shops with wifi even though they might have data on their phones or modems. The reason for this is that many of them work from home and in a country like South Africa, power can get cut off without warning. Sometimes with days stretching out into darkness. So, the restaurants and coffee shops got smart. They added wifi and power outlets for the customers to enjoy. This means that people can now get work done and no one sits at a coffee shop without ordering anything, so of course business will be good for the shop. It's nice to have a reliable source of power and internet so when wifi is down at home, you can easily go to a coffee shop and enjoy it there. Consider adding power outlets and free wifi to the list of things you offer customers. It will definitely draw attention. The power outlets are perfect because the longer their electronics last, the longer they will stay.

- Signs

Signs are meant to make people aware of certain things and enticing them. Now, this can be a difficult task if you are a new coffee shop and people don't know you very well. That is why signs are so important. They show the personality of your shop as well as the personality of your crew and the items you have on sale. Signs are a perfect way to entice people who don't know the coffee shop so keep that in mind when you are coming up with a name and a design for your sign. Font, size, and materials are important things to consider too and it will show any new customers what they can expect. It showcases your brand and personality as well! If you have an old-school coffee shop, you might want to consider using wood and white, script letters where a hipster hangout might consist of a repurposed street signs and edgier fonts.

- Layouts

You want to use the space as best as you can to utilize every nook and cranny in your building. If there is an empty corner, will a table with a single chair fit? Are the windows oddly shaped? Will some of your items that you are selling look good on window sills instead of shelves? Can you turn the counter into a sort of bar where people can sit while they wait? The layout is as important as the color scheme, if not more important. If you have a big space, you want to create the illusion that it is small and cozy and when you have a small space, you want to create one where the space looks bigger and brighter while still keeping that small café charm. Consider all of the pros and cons of every layout idea and choose the best one. Don't go into it blind. Make sure you know what the people want in a café and make sure you have clarity of exactly what you want your café to be and feel like to other people.

- In-store design

This will shape the entire mood you wish to set in the coffee shop. Dark, warm colors will make it look cozier where cold, steel greys and crisp whites will make it look clinical and bright. Or perhaps you want to add a neutral base with splashes of color, to add some charm, personality, and flair, along with showcasing local artwork and other handicraft. It's all upto you. Whatever you do with it is all up to you and your vision for the café. Remember that this is what people will associate with your coffee. Your coffee might be good but if ambience isn't appealing, they won't bother coming back any time soon. That is just something I have learned over the years. It has to have appeal to people. Choose colors and fabrics that comfort people. That makes them relax and feel at home. Choose a theme that is out of the box but something that people can still relate to.

I once helped a young woman start a book-shop/coffee shop. It was a tremendous task but I was dead set on helping her because she had the vision of a champion. Her ideas were crystal clear and she refused to settle for anything that was not a mirror image to those ideas. That is what I want to see in a business owner. Now, this woman was a writer and had a love for books that challenged any librarian. It was her passion, her entire life. I never bothered asking why she loved it so much. All I knew was that she did and that she was going to be one hell of a success because of it. Now, her vision was this; a bookshop where you can pick up any book from the shelves for a small fee and sit at the table with a nice cup of coffee while reading. At first I told her that it wasn't a bookstore, that it was a library, but then she informed me that those books were second hand and they could be sold to anyone who wanted them. She knew the struggle of finding a good book and not being able to finish it because she was reading it at a library, so she wanted to give people the option to read a bit of the book first before buying it and if they liked it, the option was there.

What really sold the place was the design she came up with. It had a charm to it that I hadn't seen in any coffee shop since. The center pieces on the tables were teacups with fresh flowers. The scent mingles with the coffee so sweetly that it was the closest thing to perfection I have ever smelled in my life. Every table had a different look, though. There were mixed and matched table cloths that gave the place a sort of nonchalant look and some tables' feet were books. Yes, actual old books that she found at a garage sale and repurposed. Those tables didn't have table cloths, and the wood of the table top was painted with rich colors that made me think of fall and hot chocolate. Every wall was lined with bookshelves that housed probably thousands of books. They were peppered with small items that were on sale. Some shelves had the in-house coffee and tea that she was selling too. Although the space was abnormally small, it didn't make me feel closed in or crowded. There were enough windows that made it just the right amount of charming. From the ceiling hung random things. The most random things I have ever seen. It was like stepping into Wonderland and having my mind blown by the pure creativeness of it all. Paintings that she has done herself hung from the high ceiling, along with crystals, a pair of shoes that resembled the ruby red ones from the Wizard of Oz, wands, scarves, and even more books seemed to float in midair. When I asked her where she got this idea, she said that it was what the inside of her mind looked like. It was chaos and she thought of all different kinds of things all at once. She compared it to Wonderland and said that she wanted to create a space where people can escape to. She knew how much people needed an escape from work or life in general. She knew what it was like to have nowhere to go. It was a space for creative minds and souls. For the artists, writers, and actors. For the poets, musicians, and crafters. As time progressed, she featured local artist's work and displayed it in the café. It was a place for the people, she said, and so the people had to be a part of it.

Customers stood outside the café before she even opened in the mornings. She had the most successful shop in town and the reason for that was that she put her heart and soul into the café. The coffee was average and the employees were tardy, but the character the place had set it apart from every other coffee shop I have ever worked with. The place had her personality written all over it and it was something the artists in town could relate with. She let them into her mind and they loved it. Even though the place was a little cluttered with books even stacked next to the register in a haphazard way, it was cozy and relaxing. It was a small artist's town and there wasn't another coffee shop around that they could go to, sit down and work in peace. They needed a place where they could be comfortable and she provided that.

The moral of this story is that you should use what you have in your arsenal and run with it, adapt it to the locals and the crowds you want to attract. If you want artists, make it artistic. If you are a painter, add some of your own pieces to the décor. The inside of the coffee shop has to set you apart from all the other coffee shops in the area. It has to be unique and charming.

- Furnishing

Deciding on furniture can be a daunting task but approached from the right angle, it can be a piece of cake. Think about what will best suit the space and style. How will the furniture help add to the character of the store? Many people believe in a uniform and matching furniture, but I have learned that it's not always the best way to go, not if you are targeting artists, anyway. It all depends on the clientele you wish to see in your café. Outfit the chairs and tables to suite people's needs. That is the best advice I can possibly give you.

There is no way to know for sure what your startup fees will be. There will be expenses that you did not calculate, or unexpected things that will happen. But you can calculate your startup fees and work with that, keeping in mind that you might have to spend more or less on whatever you are doing.

What are startup costs?

As I have mentioned, there is no possible way that you can account for everything that will cost money when you are starting out. But it is good to have a general idea and work from there. Startup costs are the costs that follow the start of your business. These are the funds that you will need and spend on equipment, furniture, your building or stand, and inventory. When you are working this out, you will get a general idea of how much money you will need to start up. It's not accurate, but it helps get an idea.

When I was in school, I hated anything that involved math. I wanted to be a businessman, not a mathematician. But I soon learned that I cannot pursue business if I can't calculate costs and percentages. Obviously I still hated it and found most of it useless and irrelevant to everyday life, but some of it stuck by me and I use it every day of my life. To this day, I cannot handle math. I despise it with every fiber of my being. Perhaps in the same way that the Evil Queen despised Snow White. That is the sort of hate I have for it. But I do not trust anyone else to do my math for me either. I'd rather take one day a week and do my own math, ensuring that everything is in order and calculated correctly than have someone else do it for me and I have to go through it later. It's tedious. So, as a lazy person when it comes to math, I have constructed a list of things to calculate in every situation to make it easier for myself. Lazy people always find the smartest way to do things, don't you agree?

What to budget for

- Equipment and furniture

This will probably be the most money you spend when starting your business, seeing as how expensive the equipment actually is. This is where you calculate how much each of the machines will cost. Remember that you will need multiple machines of a certain type in some cases, so don't forget to double or triple the costs in some of those. Also, don't go with the cheapest options either, find something mid-range or state of the art. Prices may change in the time it takes you to get the money together so rather calculate with the most expensive one and know that you are safe and won't run short on money. It's better to have extra than not enough.

- Building and utilities

When starting out, you want at least two month's rent ready, three months preferably. I often get asked why I do this and the reason is that there is no guarantee that the first few months will be profitable. There are many things to pay and many arrangements that need making. Sometimes you can either cover payroll or rent but not both. That is why you should always have a month or two's rent in the bank. That way you know that you can pay everything you need to even if you are not yet making a large profit. Rent usually takes a sizeable portion of your profit and the beginning is usually the hardest part of opening a shop. Something people also often forget about are the utilities. Electricity, gas, water, internet, and phone bills can add up to a hefty sum. It can be intimidating when you have to pay all of these, but you have rent and payroll to do as well. Try to work out how much this will be and remember to be generous. Rather have more than less. It might be hard to calculate this in the beginning as there is little to no data to go on, but after the first month you should have a clear idea of what these costs will be. Sometimes more, sometimes less, but always budget with more in mind.

- Inventory

When I first moved out, there was a big lack of groceries in my kitchen. I had a budget for what my costs would be in a month but I never bothered to calculate the exact amount of money I would need to buy everything from scratch. I had to buy everything to fill my cupboards, things that I won't need to buy every month like spices and sauces. I was so angry at myself that I gave my mother my credit card and asked her to do my shopping for me because I didn't think that far.

That is the same way it works when starting your business. You have to start from nothing to get to where you want to be. There is no coffee from last month you can use this month, no milk, no cleaning supplies. Everything is empty. Your first month's inventory expenses will be the highest it will ever be because you have to get absolutely everything. This is not the money you will need for the rest of the business' life, but it is the startup inventory cost. Make sure you account for everything and then some.

- Marketing and website

Along with math, marketing is definitely my least favorite part of any sort of business. I remember I had to make a banner to promote a local business in college. There was a whole marketing campaign about it and I can't even remember half of it. All I remember is that I absolutely hated every second of it. I even considered dropping out for that reason alone. But then I realized that I was being stupid and needed to get my act together. That doesn't make it any less tedious, though.

Where marketing is concerned, you might want to include physical materials and paid advertisement. If you are like me and arts and crafts is not your cup of tea, you might have to pay a professional to make the signs, banners, and business cards. You'll have to get a logo and ads designed for social media advertising and newspaper posts.

There is also the little thing called a website that you might be considering getting and although it is not 100% necessary, it is a useful thing to have when people want to check out what your coffee shop has to offer. Some shops even put their items that they sell in-store up for sale on their website. That way people will buy the items from all over the country and when they are in your area, would like to see what the shop looks like themselves. Which means more customers. But that has additional fees for hosting and designing as well and if you are starting small and with a small capital, you might want to skip the website for now. At least until you've made enough profit and have requests for a website. It is not necessary to make a successful business.

- Employees

Something that people like to avoid as far as possible is hiring too many employees to start off with and end up taking on more work than they can chew. The key is not to hire too few employees, but not too many to make a big dent in your money business. That is why hiring people with little to no experience is a good option as they are much cheaper to pay. Decide how many employees you will need and work out their wages, keeping legal wage minimums in mind.

- Insurance

Chances are that you invested more money in the business than you have ever done for anything else ever before. You need to protect the things you paid so much for which means you need a good insurance. Not some scam insurance company that only pays out a year after the claim has been made; you want a good one. This is definitely not something you want to skimp on. You have to protect the business just like you would your health, car, and house. Make sure you get the best business insurance you can for your specific needs.

- Taxes

Now, as it is impossible to ever know how much you will make every month, it is impossible to budget and plan for taxes. However, you can plan to get a CPA. The best thing you can do is work with a professional who will help you save money as they work out exactly what you have to deduct and what you have to pay. It is definitely worth paying a professional to do it as they will save you a lot of money in the long run. And even if you don't receive any monetary gains from it, it's okay, at least you'll have the peace of mind knowing that your taxes are up to date and perfect.

BUILDING EXCITEMENT FOR A
HUGE GRAND OPENING

*T*his lady that I mentioned with the Wonderland themed café had a knack for knowing what people want but she had one problem; she was too excitable and when it was time to open the café, she was a bundle of nerves. We had spent months preparing and investing our time into the business. There are failures that were waiting for us to make mistakes and she was starting to feel the pressure. She knew the statistics, knew that 75% of businesses failed three years into their startup phase. She was afraid of being just another statistic.

This was where I had to step in and take the reins. I had to get her excited for the opening of her café. This has been her dream since she was a child. She was supposed to be pumped and excited. Not a bundle of nerves. She was to be the face of the café and she would not make a good impression with a permanent scowl and chewed fingernails. She had to be confident.

Here's how to build excitement for your new business and how to ensure you open with a bang and not an average income.

- Pinpoint interests

Finding the target audience should be easy enough once you know exactly what to do. For example:

I want to open a rocker café. Guitars on the walls, a mural with legendary rock stars painted in their signature positions. Perhaps even a wall with photos with those rock stars with their autographs. The tables will be re-used drum sets and the chairs will be made from old, broken guitars. In the background will be a collection of rock music and live bands will perform every Friday night.

What's my target clientele? That's right, rockers and musicians. Anyone else is a bonus, but musicians are the crowd I want to attract to my shop. Once I have pinpointed that, the rest will come easy.

- How will your product change people's lives?

The only way I can possibly explain this is by giving an example.

"There is a shortage of artistic café's in the area and I have made it my mission to change that. This café will give artists the opportunity to come together and share their creative thoughts as well as find new ones in a wealthy library set up for your enjoyment."

It's short, it's sweet, and it's to the point. You aren't giving away too much but an artist's curiosity is instantly piqued. They know that they will have a community now, they will have a space to work and brainstorm. You want to make it sound as glamorous as possible, exaggerate if you must. Chances are that those artists will never even talk to one another, never mind share ideas, but it is still a space where people can get together and focus on their art. Use your dream and put it into words. In your head, artists are going to mingle and that is your goal. Advertise that. Make people want to get together. Make artists want to mingle with one another.

- Approach influencers

Another great way of advertising is through influencers. The key is to find the ones in the categories you have found the interest in. The lady with the Wonderland theme, for example, approached bookstagrammers and Booktube starts. Because her café was focused on literature and books, it seemed like the smartest thing to do and let me tell you, it was. Influencers on Youtube and Instagram have more power than you think and if they were talking about a new café that was opening with excitement, you can bet your money that people would be interested in it. Of course, there is always the chance of being shot down. Not all influencers like to advertise other people's businesses on their channels but it only takes one influencer to get back to you to make the whole project blow up much bigger than you ever anticipated. That being said, you want the right sort of influencer to promote your product. With the scandals going on in the beauty community, you wouldn't want James Charles to promote your cosmetics store. Not because of anything he may or may not have done, but because there is too much bad publicity surrounding him. Find the influencers who have a good reputation.

- Social media

Social media is your best friend. When I compare the modern day and age to when I was a child, it seems like two completely different worlds. Nowadays, elementary school students have cellphones. It has taken over the world. The internet is everywhere and you won't get to a house where there is no wifi.

That just doesn't happen. This can be used to your advantage. We are all so used to social media, why not use that to your advantage? You are on your phone most of the day anyway, use that to advertise your café. Don't be afraid to use what you are good at. Use those fast fingers to type out a quick advertisement and post them on groups and pages. I'm talking about Instagram, Twitter, Facebook and even YouTube if you feel particularly brave. Honestly, the world is your oyster when it comes to social media marketing so use that to your and your business's advantage. Everyone is on social media, which means everyone will see it.

- Giveaways and contests

My sister has the terrible habit of entering every competition she sees. It doesn't even matter what it is for. She only does it because she loves free things. That was when I realized that people eat it up, especially women. They enjoy the thrill of a competition and giveaway and that is exactly what you want. You want to appeal to people. A perfect example of this is putting an ad on Facebook and having the contestants tag a certain amount of friends in the post. These posts usually spread like wildfire and all you have to do is sit back and watch without doing anything else. It will only cost a coupon for ten free coffees, or perhaps a collection of craft coffees. It doesn't have to cost much. People enjoy things that they do not have to pay for, no matter how cheap or stupid it might be. The Wonderland woman hosted a giveaway. The prize was a collection of classics. The books came from her own bookshelves and she has been wanting to get rid of it for ages. They were collector's editions which makes it valuable. She had no use for it so she created a use for it. This also gave some clues as to what the café will be like and what she will be offering. Two birds with one stone.

- Suspense

Like any good showman, it is important to keep your audience in suspense. The point of this is to make people curious for your products and the unveiling of the café. I have gone on and on about marketing, and you might ask, "But Alex, how am I supposed to build suspense if I have to market?" The answer is simple. Marketing isn't supposed to be about your product; it's about what it can do for people. It's about what it might be able to do. It's not showing the potential customers what your café is going to look like; it's how you create a vision by saying, "It is going to be a place for artists to come together." That is enough. You don't have to say anything else on the topic. They know enough and to build suspense, you have to figure out how much is too much and how little is too little. You want to advertise small, random parts of the business, not the entire thing. This is a sort of romance. There has to be at least a little bit of mystery to keep the flame alive. The flame being the public's curiosity in this instance.

PUTTING IT ALL TOGETHER - HOW TO MAKE A FULL BUSINESS PLAN

*T*he term "business plan" is enough to make anyone's blood turn to ice. Unfortunately, every business needs a written business plan. It is not as intimidating as it sounds, and I am here to help you through it and put everything you've worked on together to make one banging business plan.

According to SBA.gov, every business plan should contain the following.

- Executive summary

Here, you basically write why your company will succeed and why it is going to be unique. This is also where you should add some information about management and your leadership team.

- Company description

Don't be afraid to go into detail when describing your company and what it does to solve certain problems. This is the way you want other people to describe your company. Don't be afraid to boast a little. Be descriptive, but avoid being boring.

- Market analysis

You have experience in being a barista or managing a coffee shop, use that information. You know the market and that is what you have to show your reader. Do some research concerning the market and competitors. Also add why your company will be able to compete with other leading companies in the same area.

- Organization and management

Who will manage your café? Will it be you or will you be hiring someone? Who will take over when you are not around? Inform your reader about the legal structure of your business and where you see it in the future. Will it be part of a chain or a single café? You can also use charts to help convey your point.

- Service or product

Tell the reader about everything you will be serving and offering at the stand or café. Why is this going to be popular?

- Marketing and sales

How are you going to attract customers? Also add a section where you explain how your sales strategy will work and how you are going to approach a customer.

- Funding request

I will advise against any funding in general, but if there is no other way, this is where you will mention how much funding you will need to start your business. How long will it take you to pay the debt back?

- Financial projections

This is where you have to convince your reader that your coffee shop is going to be successful. You want to convince then that your business will be stable and if you are looking for funding, they will want to know that you will be able to pay them back.

- Appendix

This is completely optional, but it is useful to add

things like credit histories, letters of references, permits, legal documents, and resumes.

Now that you know what an average business plan should look like, here are some tips to help you with this project.

- Do enough research and make sure it's legitimate

If you want to construct a good business plan, you have to do the right research and make sure that it is legitimate. It's easy enough to get info from Wikipedia, but the chances of that information being accurate isn't high enough for you to trust it 100% of the time. The best thing to do is exploring different information sources, perhaps even going to the library to double-check some facts. You have to know your business, your product, market and competition inside and out. It is your responsibility to educate the reader and to do that, you have to have your facts lined up and proven. You can't say something like: "Coffee is the most consumed beverage in the world." That's not true. There are things that is much more popular than coffee and once your reader sees that even one of your facts isn't 100% accurate, then you will have a tough time convincing them that everything else you've given them is. Take some more time constructing your business plan instead of jumping into it blindly. Do all the research you possibly can.

- Company profile

What is it that your company does? What are you offering the public? What is the history of the company and what makes your coffee shop unique? A good example of company profiles is scanning their website for an 'About' page. There you will find everything you need to know about the company, their history and the services they offer. This profile has the potential to draw in new customers, so make sure that it is good and entertaining.

Personally, if I read an about page and there is nothing interesting, I lose interest and move on to something else. I want to be entertained so entertain me!

- Marketing

Any good business plan has a good and well thought through business plan in place. These marketing plans have to be strategic, smart and maybe even a little aggressive. Show the reader that you mean business. You want to make sure that they know you are in it for the long run and by investing all that time in a marketing strategy will prove it. This strategy has to include ways to introduce your existing products to the public as well as introducing new ones. It also has to boost your sales, refining products, enhance the available services and products, advertisement plans and extending your business.

- Appeal to investors

Do you know those advertisements with the car salesman making buying a car seem so incredibly easy? You know, the ones where he smiles at the end and his tooth twinkles? Okay, now imagine yourself in that position. You want to be that guy. You want to be the person that makes things look appealing to potential investors. That is the idea of your business plan. You want to appeal to people, to convince them that the data you've gathered is good, solid, and perfect for a for them to invest in your business. When you are appealing to investors, you want to talk numbers. Honestly, they don't care about what you do to come up with the money, as long as you do. You could be selling old hardcover dustjackets and they wouldn't care. All they care about is the money you are going to earn by doing that, you are earning them money. See where I'm going with this? Appeal to them with the numbers and the promise of a lot of it. Everything starting with expenses to profits. They want to see everything. Don't leave anything to the imagination. If the numbers look attractive, don't be shy to add then.

- What's the actual purpose of this plan?

But not everyone wants investors. In fact, I have worked with more startup businesses that refused the help of investors than those that actually accepted it. I encourage this, but if you do need funding and investors, you need to set out to get their attention. If you are funding this project yourself, the business plan will have a different look and feel to it because you are not focusing so much on money and rather the purpose of your business and how it can appeal to the everyday person.

- Why are you suitable for this position of power?

In this business plan, you also want the reader to be convinced that you are suitable for the role. You have to tell them why you think you have what it takes to open a business and make it work. You have to show them that you have the credentials and have done the research. Prove to them that you know the market inside and out, that no one can tell you anything about coffee.

If infuriates me when people want to start a business but don't know their own products. It really makes me angry because if you don't know the product or market, what is it that makes you suitable for this position. I love people who can go out of their way and are passionate about what they want and why they want to do it. If you are passionate about coffee, it is ten times more appealing to a customer than an owner who doesn't know a coffee bean from a tea leaf. I want you to think of me as the reader and then surprise me with your commitment and passion. Convince me that your coffee is going to be the best in town because you actually know what you are talking about.

- Who will you be presenting your business plan to?

Much like the purpose of the plan, you want to sit down and think about who you are going to give this plan to. Perhaps you are just out of high school and want to convince your parents that you can do this. Maybe you are going to the bank, investors or any other official you might need help and permission from. Passion is not going to appeal to certain investors or banks, but it will sit well with your parents if it's paired with good numbers. If you have to create ten different business plans to hand out to different people, do it. It can only help you.

BRANDING SECRETS

*W*hen I was a kid, I refused to buy anything that wasn't branded. Don't get me wrong, I wasn't some rich kid who had a thousand dollars every day to spend on useless things. I worked for every penny I had. And I spent those pennies on things that I could have gotten much cheaper somewhere else with the same quality. I suppose at the time, my mind worked differently. I wanted to fit in. I'd rather have Gucci sneakers than Walmart ones and that is how people tend to think in today's day an age as well. They'd rather buy a branded product than an unbranded one. For example, there's a reason why Starbucks has such a big and loyal fanbase. It's definitely not because of their overpriced coffee, I can tell you that much. It's because they have this name that everyone associates with the upper-class people. You see celebs walking around with a Starbucks cup, every YouTuber talks about it and that pulls the 'normal' folk in. It makes people feel as if they can be a part of something that those stars are a part of. This is why a lot of small businesses fold after a year or two. They just can't compete with the unlimited marketing budgets and loyal customers that keep going back even though their products are trash.

This means that you will have to work double as hard on your marketing strategies and building your brand. Luckily for you, you have me to help you with that.

But before we get into the fun stuff, we need to have a look at what a brand is exactly.

A brand is your reputation. It's as simple as that. Starbucks has the reputation of being loved by celebrities and that is part of their brand. It is what people say about you when you are not in the room. It's what people associate with you and your products. Remember when I said that you should get in contact with an influencer? Here is the why. If you get a famous person to promote your brand, people will look at your coffee shop and think, "Hey, Instagram model loves this place. That means it should be pretty good." That is just how it works. People tend to try new things because other people influenced them to do so. Do you follow? This is also why getting the right sort of influencer is important because they will be associated with your shop.

Now, the question remains; how do I build a brand?

- Target Clientele

There is a wealth of ways you can build your brand and the first step to do this is through determining your target audience. Now you need to study their lifestyle and decide what the best approach to creating a brand will be. Here are a few examples from the top of my head (note that I will be naming famous influences that might never even respond to requests but for the sake of the example, I am going ahead and doing it anyway).

Artists love art channels on YouTube. I'm talking Jazza, Vex, and Bayley Jae.

Millennials worship David Dobrik and his vlog squad.

Gamers and tech enthusiasts will be interested when someone like Pewdiepie or Jacksepticeye is connected to your brand.

I can go on and on, but you get my point. A metal head won't have any idea who Jazza is if they are not interested in art so why should they even give your metal themed café a go because who is this weirdo promoting their brand?

It also depends on the ages you wish to attract as well as a number of other things. Here is a list of things you have to consider before starting your branding campaign because without knowing these things, you will definitely attract the wrong crowd and your entire vision will be down the drain.

Age

Male, female or gender neutral

Location

Income

Interests

Style

Influences

- Brands associated with these people

While you are narrowing your target audience down, you might realize that you had nothing to worry about with the Starbucks across the street because you are targeting a different clientele. Also, narrowing this down gives you a very good idea of what online marketing and ads you have to target.

- A mission statement

What is that? Well, I'm glad you asked.

A mission statement is the statement a company makes. This is different from a tag-line. An example of a mission statement is that of Starbucks. "To inspire and nurture the human spirit–one person, one cup and one neighborhood at a time."

Now, I am not a Starbucks fan, but that statement alone makes me want to pay them a visit and throw my money at them. With a statement like that, they target a wide range of customers. Every person has a spirit, every person lives in a neighborhood. That is the sort of mission statement you want to have. You want to target people, make them want to visit your shop. "We provide that fuel to your creative mind." Are you telling me that an artist will walk past a coffee shop with such a mission state-ment and not be at least a little curious? There is no way of that happening. That is your goal. Make it irresistible and catchy. Make it feel as if every person is being targeted individually while you are actually addressing the masses.

- Research your competitors and their brands

Yes, friends, unfortunately there is more research to be done. You want to research and analyze your competitor's brand. If they have been around for years and years, their brand obviously works for them. Take lessons from them and write things down what comes to mind when you are reading their tag-line or mission statement. What does it make you feel? *That* is the feeling you want to mimic with your own brand. If they aren't doing so well, try to figure out what they aren't doing right.

- Identify the things a good brand name is

It's easy for customers to identify as a certain company's brand. A good brand is also short and catchy; something that people will remember. You want a good reputation because that is what's going to be a good brand.

- Create a logo

Remember that banner I told you about that I absolutely hated making? That was nothing compared to coming up with logos for make-believe companies. It always seemed to be copied from something I don't even remember seeing. It was a horrible experience.

I have found that hiring a professional to do this is the best possible option. Sit down with him or her and discuss what you want in the logo. You want it to be simple and eye-catching. You want it to appeal to your target clientele. Musical instruments for musicians, books for book lovers, paints and brushes for artists. Make sure that your coffee shop's personality shines through the logo as well.

The Wonderland coffee shop had a rabbit mask on a pile of books and a cup of coffee. It was cute and it caught people's attention as soon as they saw it. It showed the personality of the café as well as the things it offered its customers. I will always use it as a perfect example.

- Create a tag-line

One of the more difficult things to come up with if you ask me. Especially since there are so many good one out there. "Just do it" for Nike. "Always low prices. Always" for Walmart and "Adidas is all in" for Adidas. Those tag-lines are catchy and you will do well to take some notes. You want something that will get stuck in people's heads.

- Find a voice

Above all else, you want your brand to find a voice. You want to be relevant. This won't come easy and I am not going to lie to you about there being many trials and errors. You have to test the waters and find a platform where you will have the best voice. If you say something, you want people to pay attention. You want to talk to your clients through your brand. Wendy's, for example, has the whole Twitter thing where they roast their followers. That is their voice. People engage in it and you want people to engage in your posts as well. Speak up and announce your arrival. To do this, you have to use your brand wherever you are.

- Use your brand

Much like the iconic Starbucks cup, you want to have something that people instantly associate with you. Your logo or tag-line has to be on everything. If customers walk into your coffee shop, your logo has to be on display. Put your logo on a stamp pad, and stamp everything you can get your hands on. Packaging, advertisements, everything. It has to be as visible as possible.

- Advertisement

Finally, you need to advertise your brand. No one is going to hear about you if you do not tell them. Flyers, pop-ups, newspaper articles, YouTube, television ads and social media. Plaster it everywhere and never stop. Don't stop when you get customers and rely on word-of-mouth. You want as many people as possible to know about you so make sure you yell it from the rooftops.

DREAM CLIENT SECRET- SO YOU CAN HAVE MASS AMOUNTS OF YOUR FAVORITE PEOPLE

*W*e've already handled getting to your target 'audience' in earlier chapters, so I'll be quick with this guide to define things a little.

Let's take a look at what a target market is and why it's important.

A target market is the concentrated group of consumers that you wish to sell your product or service to. Walmart's target market is people on a budget that can get good deals at good prices. The Dollar Store is directed toward lower income people who have to save money wherever they can. Your target market will be coffee lovers, but you have to define that a little further. What sort of coffee lovers? What social group do you intend on having at your coffee shop and why? Hipsters, for example, love fancy, imported coffees. From personal experience, business people enjoy straight up black coffee and although you might intend on providing both, you want something to specialize in. Something that makes you stand out from your competitors and to do that you need to know what your customers would want. It's a cycle. You can't do one without the other and the beginning of the cycle is knowing who your customers will be and what they would like to see in your coffee shop. This also helps with advertising as you will then know exactly where to advertise and market for the most effective results. Book lovers, for example, will be more likely to see ads near libraries and bookstores than at the stadium.

Here are a few tips to identify your target market and how to focus on it.

- Start at the beginning

There are two ways of approaching this step. You can either determine what you will be selling, or you can decide what your target market will be and construct your menu accordingly.

So, you are going to sell coffee. What kind of coffee will you be serving? Is it going to be vegan? Will you serve light meals too and if you are, what kind? Will it be comfort food with rich flavors and steamy sides or salads and healthy sandwiches? What are your customers' characteristics? What problems will you be solving with your coffee shop? Will it be a hangout spot or a quick grab 'n go stand? These are all aspects you have to take into consideration when you are determining your target market.

The second option is my favorite.

See, I have a set idea in my head. I can imagine the coffee shop in front of me. I can see the leather jackets and tattoos of the rockers I wish to see in my rocker café. I can see the musicians in the corner working on songs and I can see the piercings glint when the light touches them in just the right way. My target audience will be rockers. And I will solve the problem of limited hangouts for this group of people by giving them a new, cool and fresh one, welcoming them all. I will adjust my menu accordingly to that because I don't want any other crowd hanging around there. They are my vision and I have to decide on things that will attract them to my coffee shop. It's up to you. The decision comes down to what you find important; the crowd or the coffee?

- What is in demand?

Some people don't care about the menu or the customers. All they care about is making money and running their business to their full potential. That isn't a bad thing at all. Now, if this is you, you want to figure out what is popular in your area. What is in demand? What do people want to see? If your goal is to attract every local around, you want to know what there is a shortage of and how people will respond to you introducing it to them. Who will benefit most from your business being opened? Those are the people you want to target. You want to target those that it will benefit the most. It's close to impossible to make everyone happy, but this is a way to widen your target market up a bit. These are general statistics regardless of age or social groups. You will merely be serving those that benefit the most from your shop and coffee. Perhaps that market will be businessmen who will prefer your coffee shop for meetings over any other place. If there aren't many venues around, that is a very likely thing that will happen, and it will benefit them the most. That will be your target market, then.

- Study the customers that are most likely to visit your coffee shop before focusing on a new target

If you open your store in the middle of town, surrounded by other businesses, chances are that your main clientele will be the employees of those businesses. In the beginning, it is important to attract anyone you possibly can to your store.

I once worked with a man who opened a coffee

shop dead center in an industrial area. It was a plain little shop with nothing special besides cheap and affordable beverages and lunches. He was smart. He created a menu that was cheap enough for the average person to afford every day. Some of his meals were even cheaper than what a person could make at home without the trouble of actually having to do it. He knew that his main market will be the employees at first. They will visit his coffee shop, looking for a quick meal and beverages for lunch and he used it to his advantage. He started with what would satisfy them.

Sooner or later, the companies began taking their clients to the coffee shop for meetings and those customers returned every time they visited the company they were seeing. The owner was a magician with coffee and experimented with muffins that complimented every single beverage on the menu. People found it charming and his products were undeniably delicious. He used the employees of other companies to lure more people in and once that started happening, he expanded his menu to suit everyone's needs. He hardly even needed marketing because people were doing it for him. All because he was approaching the business in a smart and logical way. He knew that in the location he was in, he wasn't going to attract anyone else and he used it to his advantage. Be smart.

- Who do your competitors target?

Another good way to determine a target market is discovering who your competitors are targeting and there are two ways you can approach this. You can either target the same market, keeping in mind that the fight for customers will be tooth and nail, or you can target a different market that does not have a company that targets them yet.

If you decide on targeting the same market, know that your competitors will not go down without a fight. They also have a loyal customer base before you can even get moved into your building. Profits may also not be as high because you will be sharing customers. The positive thing is that you will know the market is active in the area seeing as your competitors have stayed open for so long.

Targeting a different market will ensure that you are the only coffee shop they will visit seeing as you are the only one to cater to their needs. This is what I always encourage people to do but there are risks. As good as having the market all to yourself, there is no way of knowing how well the market will go. There is no way of knowing just how much money you will make. The market may only have two customers which will make sharing a market the better option. But in the case that you target the right one, profits will be significantly better than sharing. Do some research about the markets in the area and make sure that you know what you are doing. You are not going to open a toy store in an old-age-home. If the profitable markets in the area are not the ones you are looking for, perhaps it's time to relocate or change your idea of the ideal market.

- Expanding

Once you have hooked one market, what is keeping you from hooking another one? Who says you can't expand your brand to different markets as well? The key to successfully doing this is not changing what you already have so you lose your current customer base, but to add to it to attract new, different people.

If I ever opened that rock café, my goal would be to get punks and metal heads in there as well. This means I will have to adjust the music I play to accommodate them all and advertising at different locations as well. If I want to attract more people, I might have to add to my menu as well to appeal to them.

It should be your goal to expand and become more popular. Whether it's in the one target market of four others, your goal shouldn't be to stay one size. Your profits should increase every year and the only way you are going to do that is by expanding. IF you make the same profits every year, it'll be as if you are losing money thanks to the economy. You have to grow as life becomes more expensive.

If you know what your target is, it is easy to add to the menu and take away, add to the shop and take away, even adjust your own staff.

MARKETING SECRETS: HAVE RELIABLE INCOME MONTH TO MONTH

As I have said before, you can't stop marketing once you have opened. You have to keep the marketing going as long as possible. There has to be some sort of advertisement going on at all times. You have to remind people of your coffee shops' existence. Remember those bangin' espressos? Well, we are back with new flavors! Remind them of what they loved in the first place and then improve on that. You don't want to stay the same, boring coffee shop for the rest of its life. But changes need to be announced and that is where marketing comes in.

But, chances are that you do not have the necessary funding for such things. Especially since you have spent most of your money on marketing before opening. It takes a few months for your business to find its footing completely and until you can afford professional marketing again, here are a few things that you can do with a limited budget. These methods are effective enough, if not just as effective as professional marketing.

- The guerrilla method

This is a method that small companies use to compete with bigger ones. Where big companies rely on money for their marketing, guerrilla marketing relies on creativity and originality. When I first heard of this method I thought that is was utter rubbish. How can anything compete with money? But upon further investigation, I found that it is truly a brilliant way of marketing. When I was doing the Wonderland café, the owner refused to do any traditional marketing as that wasn't the crowd she wanted to attract. She wanted artists and readers and what better way than to advertise artistically? Here are a few ideas. Remember that the key is in creativeness. The goal is to find the most artistic way to advertise

Have people go undercover. Oh yes, go James Bond on the streets. It might be a little bit cheating but if it works, it works. For a small fee, you have people go undercover on the street as customers and rave about your products. When I did some further research, I found that Sony did a similar thing. They paid people to go undercover on the streets and have strangers take photos of them with their Sony cameras. That way, the person got a taste of the camera and the undercover agent made a show of raving about the camera. Smart, Sony. Very sneaky, but incredibly smart.

Instead of hiring a professional designer to design a billboard of some sort, get a brick and mortar location and get an artist to create some art on it. Artists will be drawn to this as it is hand-painted and a lot of effort went into it. It appeals to people more than corporate billboards do. It's definitely something to consider even when marketing before opening. You will pay less money for an artist to paint a wall than a designer to design billboards and having them set up.

- Social media

Keep the social media active. It doesn't help if you were active on social media before opening and then letting it die afterward. You can even hire people to manage your accounts for you. Keep the advertisement going and get your followers to participate in your posts.

- Expand your horizons

So you have started on social media but where do you go from there? Where can you possibly expand to? Well, let me tell you that people love other methods of marketing as well. Blog posts, YouTube videos, podcasts, and even pop-ups. Do some research and determine what will best attract the attention of your target clientele. Most of these methods cost little to nothing and it's what attracts a lot of people. It's definitely very effective.

- Take advantage of the media

If you want free marketing, milking the media is the way to go. Anything you do is going to be costly in one way or another, but there are ways to get featured on media for 'free' advertising. Things such as publicity stunts can increase your chances of being featured. Remember that time Richard Branson dressed up as a female flight attendant on his own airline? Now that was a publicity stunt. Another way you can achieve this is through sponsoring your local football team or entering a business contests. Do giveaways and make sure everyone knows about it. There is a wealth of things you can do to get publicity and that and you are only limited by your imagination. Once you are featured, your name will be out in the world and that is your goal achieved. You might even want to try organizing interviews for the media. Many newspapers like to interview small, up-and-coming businesses and showing support for their local entrepreneurs. All you have to do is find the right one.

- Charity work

I'm a firm believer in helping people without expecting anything in return, but as fate would have it, helping people is a great marketing method. For example, if someone has a burger joint they might want to hand out burgers to homeless people after leaking it to the press. A toy store might visit orphanages and hand out toys for Christmas. Not only do you help the people that really need it, but you are also getting publicity for it. Donating to charity is also a great way to market but it costs a lot and as a start-up business, you might not have those funds to do it. The Wonderland café took to the streets and handed out books to whoever would take it. She didn't leak it to the media, but somehow news got out and it spread like wildfire. She even took the time to sit down and read to kids who couldn't read themselves. Small things like that will win you the favor of the locals as well as give you a fantastic reputation. You honestly can't go wrong with charity work and I encourage this with every business I help.

DAY TO DAY OPERATIONS

So you have opened your coffee stop, hired employees, and got the grand opening you always dreamed about. Now what?

Now, my friend, now the real work begins.

Opening a coffee shop is the easy part, keeping it open is the hard bit. It's your job to run things, to make sure everything is in order for your employees. You are the big boss now and your employees will look up to you for guidance and leadership. Here are some things that you will have to do now that your coffee shop is up and running and some tips to do those things.

- Keep track of cash flow

At the end of the day, everything is about money. The goal of your business is to make money and it's what keeps your business running. You have to keep track of the money coming in and leaving the store, make sure that you are making a profit and that you are prepared for anything that might happen that'll need a big chunk of money to fix or replace. If you have followed my advice and have a few months' rent stocked up, that'll be one less problem to worry about. These months will give you the chance to study the business and discover what the cash flow is like. You have to be sure that you can afford rent once you've run out of backup money. These months will give you the opportunity to work on your business and help it grow enough to cover all of the costs easily and effectively.

Another thing you will have to do is enter and organize financial information into a ledger of some sorts and handle payroll. It's important to keep everything organized and at hand whenever you need it.

- Restocking inventory

As resources get used, the inventory will drop, and it will need constant restocking. But you can't just restock it without keeping tabs on the inventory and monitoring what gets used and what is needed. You might not have to be the one to manage the purchasing department, but it is your business after all. You have to keep track of things.

- Employees

Arguably the most important part of your business, your employees have to be looked after and taken care of. With employees come human resources responsibilities and a mountain of paperwork. Once the business is up and running, you might need more personnel, so you'll have to hire more people and have them trained. You'll also have to train your existing personnel.

There is tax information that you need to track as well as all legal documentation.

Going in the complete opposite direction of finances, you have to be the one to take disciplinary action wherever it might be needed and address employee complaints and concerns. Basically, you have to take care of your employees and make sure that their working environment encourages them to work harder. Employees work harder when they know that they have a boss who takes care of them and goes the extra mile. It will motivate them to walk that extra mile for you as well.

- Make profit

Your main goal as a business is to earn money. You can say what you want, but without profit, there is no business that needs running. You have to ensure that your business is making enough profit to cover all of the costs the coffee shop has. At first, I advise that you be personally responsible for this part of the business. You can hire people for that position later, but the first couple of months, you need to get an idea of the business' finances and where you can cut or have to add a little. If you are not making a profit, you have to reprice the items on your menu because that is your sole income. That is what has to bring the money in. Either that or you have to serve a much bigger crowd which will be difficult if you have a small space to begin with. Now that the business is open, you have to keep the profit coming in order for it to stay open. Otherwise the entire venture is useless.

- Customers

Customers bring the money in and it's your job to take care of them in the same way that you take care of your staff. You have to take care of the customers' needs and listen to their special requests. Special requests equal money, so try your best to make that happen. It's also important that you work with the customer through the sales process as well as listen to their suggestions and concerns.

Customer feedback is a great way to know what the public is thinking about you. You want the people to come back to you and tell you what they loved and what they hated, which parts they would return for and which parts put them off entirely.

On social media, if the customer has feedback, you have to respond to them. As with everything else, you can easily hire someone for the job but at first you might want to do it yourself. People love an owner who is hands-on and knows what they are talking about.

- Marketing

I feel like every chapter involves me mentioning marketing on one way or the other.

Marketing is very important even once the company is open. It's important to keep new faces coming and getting the word out there. It doesn't have to be as aggressive as when you were marketing before opening, but it can't come to a standstill. You have to reinforce your brand and keep it strong. Create a marketing budget as well as managing advertisements and company branding.

You are the one who has to arrange competitions and giveaways to keep people interested and even if you do have a marketing team, they will still need your permission for these things. It's time to make big decisions as every decision has a consequence the business will have to face so keep the marketing and branding positive.

HOW TO DEAL WITH RUDE CUSTOMERS

*L*et me tell you a little story about the rudest customer I have ever had in my entire life.

As a teen working at a local coffee shop, I had no patience for rude customers. I had my own things I was going through as a teen. My girlfriend just dumped me for a football player and my parents refused to get me a drum set for Christmas. My life couldn't get any worse, or at least that was what it felt like. My life was falling apart, and it was playing out exactly like one of those cheesy teenage movies. It frustrated me.

My parents forced me to get a job because I was making them miserable and they thought I could use something to take my mind off things. My aunt ran a local coffee shop and my parents managed to convince her to hire me even though she wasn't short-staffed. I tried my best to get out of it, of course. As a teenage boy there was no way that I was going to be cool in school if I was working at a coffee shop, and at that stage, I was determined to become the most popular kid in school to win my girlfriend back. I was such an idiot back then, but it seemed like a great idea.

Now, after months of working at the coffee shop and when I finally accepted that this would be my after-school routine for a good year or two, a woman walked in with the most sour face I have ever seen. She had a phone pressed to her ear and eyed the customers up and down with a look of utter disgust. I knew her as the mother of the football player who stole my girlfriend. I instantly hated the woman.

Pulling myself from the counter I was leaning against where I was talking to a girl from school who suffered the same fate of being forced into work, I strode over to the customer and gave her my biggest, most fake smile. I assumed it was something terrible because she cringed and then rolled her eyes at me. I took her order as fast as I could, wanting this woman out of the café as soon as possible. She was making the other customers uncomfortable and when they were uncomfortable, we had to suffer their wrath. I was not in the mood for any of that.

So, I made her coffee and handed it to her.

I should have warned her that it was hot; I really should have. And I shouldn't have been grinning when she took a sip and burned her mouth. I've never heard a woman use the sort of language that she spat in my direction at that moment. I was torn between laughing and hiding under the counter. The entire café was looking at me.

"You idiot boy," she said, her nostrils flaring. "Why is it so hot?"

In that moment, anger boiled inside of me like a volcano. It was busy erupting and There were three ways I could've gone about it. I could have apologized and offered her a refund, I could have yelled right back at her and told her how bad her haircut was, or I could have smiled at her while making a snarky comment. I knew better than to do the latter, but it didn't stop me. She was humiliating me, as if her son hadn't done enough damage.

"It's coffee, lady. If you wanted it to be cold, you should have ordered a milkshake."

She was furious and to be honest, so was I. I was ready to face any consequences that came my way. Anything was worth seeing the look on her face. I wished that she burned enough so she wouldn't be able to talk for a few days.

Unfortunately, that didn't happen, and she demanded that I get fired or she would drag the café's name through the mud all over town. As one of the wealthiest women in town, she had the power to do a lot of damage.

My aunt fired me on the spot.

Long story short, my aunt told me that she was a total jerk to everyone in town, but that didn't mean I could put the café's reputation in danger. I understood that.

Something I learned at a very young age was that a customer is always right. No matter how rude they are, no matter what they say to people, they are always right. The customer holds all the power and as a business owner, you rely on a good word from your customers. You rely on having a good reputation and you need them to promote your business as far as possible. Even one client that refuses to visit your shop is a loss. But there are different ways to handle different situations. Sometimes a customer is unhappy and might across as rude or vice versa.

Here are a few tips and tricks to deal with rude and unhappy customers.

- The sorting hat

Firstly, you have to be able to discern between a rude customer from an unhappy customer. Rude customers are mean because they can be. They feel invincible and empowered when entering a store because they know that no one can touch them. The customer is always right, and they know it. They know that employees and owners will do whatever it takes to keep them happy and that makes them uncivil and difficult.

Unhappy customers have reason to be unhappy and they can't control their emotions a lot of the time. They might come across as rude, but they really aren't. They might only be disappointed in what they were served or even the service.

Once you know what sort of customer you are dealing with, it's easier to handle the situation but regardless of what they are, you have to keep them happy at all costs. Knowing that an unhappy customer is unhappy and not rude will make controlling your emotions much easier and when you know the customer is rude, you are aware that you have to work extra hard to keep your anger at bay.

- Control your emotions

This is probably the hardest thing to do when someone is being unnecessarily rude or hurtful. I have a terrible temper and I struggle with this daily. Once you let your emotions take control over you instead of you controlling your emotions, things will get ugly. That is when you don't care about what you say anymore, and it can land you in some hot water. Keeping your cool around a rude customer will keep your employees calm as well but as soon as you burst into flames while and start raging, so will your employees. You are the leader and you have to stay calm and collected. Most of the time it isn't fair, and people are just looking to cause trouble, but this is your business, the baby you have raised from nothing. Talking back to one rude customer is not worth risking all your hard work.

- Fight fire with water

Fighting fire with fire will only cause a bigger fire to erupt and it will burn down everything in the close vicinity. If your client is shouting at you, keep quiet and nod. Don't shout back and don't throw insults around. A person will be tempted to roll their eyes or suck on a tooth but the key is to stay as calm as you possibly can and wait for the customer to finish before calmly offering a refund or an apology on behalf of the guilty party.

- Step in

When you see a customer attacking an employee, don't hesitate to step in. This is your property and your business. They are making a scene in your space so it's your right to step in and sort it out. It's your duty. Employees are easily flustered sometimes and can't handle the wrath of some customers so be the leader that you are and step in. it will also show the customers that you are not afraid to step in and take responsibility. You are the one who employed these people and you are the one offering your services to customers. Stepping in to calm the storm is always a must. If your employee is in the wrong, have him apologize and handle the rest in private. Don't give them a warning in front of everyone else, instead lead them to the back and talk to them.

- It's not always personal

People say things that they don't mean all the time but it's hard not to take things personally all the time. Remember that they are angry, and angry people don't always know what they are saying. They don't know you and they don't know the things you've faced or struggled with. If they shout at you and the insult hits home, it's only coincidence. Nothing more. They will throw insults until they hit a nerve, so don't take it personally.

- Apologize, but stay firm if appropriate

Always apologize to a customer but you don't have to grovel. Apologize and offer a free coffee or a refund. You don't have to beg for forgiveness if they don't accept your peace offering. They might act like royalty, but they have no power over you. Don't be rude, yet still stand your ground. If the customer is factually wrong, you don't have to say that you were the one in the wrong. Some people need an assertive hand for things to sink in. You don't want to be known as the coffee shop owner who lets anyone walk over them. "The customer is always right" doesn't mean that the customer is always right in every instance. It just means that you have to be the bigger person and try to make amends. If they don't want to accept it, honestly, there isn't much more you can do so don't beg.

- Try to solve the problem

If the customer got cold food or the wrong cup of coffee, fix it as soon as possible. Perhaps even tell them that it's on the house. A lot of times these things get out of hand because the owner or manager isn't willing to solve the problem.

- Train your staff

A good idea is to train your staff in dealing with customers. It might be a costly process but getting them trained properly is a very good way to ensure that drama is avoided as much as possible and it will give you peace of mind knowing that it's not your staff's fault. If you can't afford training just yet, perhaps do it yourself or lay down some house rules. Make sure they know what you know about handling customers. It's a good alternative.

THE ACCOUNTING AND TAX GUIDE

Accounting
What is accounting?

Accounting is the study of your business. It's your business' way of talking to you. Of telling you what's wrong and what's going right. There is no room for lying where accounting is involved and it makes it easy for you as a business owner to know where exactly your business is standing. Some would say that accounting is the language of money and I fully agree with it. Accounting answers all of the following questions and then some.

- Is the company making money and how much is it making?
- How deep is the company in debt?
- Where is the dead weight?

- Is there money to invest and expand?
- Is it necessary to invest and expand?
- How much money is owed to the business?
- Which months are more profitable?
- Are we losing money?
- How much money does the company need to run every month?
- What are the expenses?

All of these questions are crucial ones to ask in a business whether you are only starting out or are already a well-established coffee shop. Accounting is also very important when it comes to taxes so there is no way you can get out of doing taxes. Types of financial statement users

Aside from the necessary people in your business, there are external people that also need a certain amount of financial information on your company. Of course there are things that you should never share or to certain people, so here are the main people who need information and why they need it.

- Creditors

One word: creditibility. Creditors and lenders need to know that you are accountable and will pay them back responsibly for the amount you want to borrow from them. You are not going to let a friend borrow money from you if you don't know exactly what for or know that they will never going to pay you back. This is business and they have to be certain that you are using it for the right things and that you can pay them back when the time comes.

- Shareholders and investors

These people need to be certain that they are not investing all of their money into a dead-end business. How will they know this? By looking at the books of the business. If you are not making money, what use do they have in investing in your company? Why buy shares if the company is going to fail sooner rather than later?

- Suppliers

If you are not paying for everything in cash, your suppliers will need the proper information to judge whether or not you will be able to pay them back if they extend your credit. They need to know that you are capable of using the products you bought from them to earn enough from it again to pay them back. Many people can't, and try getting credit extensions as a last resort. It is perfectly understandable that they need proof that you will be able to repay them. They will be the ones who are working at a loss if they do not get what is owed to them, and no company can afford that.

- Regulators and unions

Regulators make sure that businesses follow the applicable laws and to do this, the need access to your financial statements. These regulators make monitor companies in an attempt to reduce fraud between businesses. They are not to be confused with the IRS who focuses on Tax.

Unions, on the other hand, ensure that you are paying your employees fairly based on your financial information.

Both of these organization types make sure that there is no fraud taking place within your business. It can also benefit you when other businesses might be taking you for a ride of their own.

- Press

When your company grows, the press will need your financial information in order to report your financial status. This, however, only happens when you become relevant enough in their world which won't happen for a good year or two, or ever. They mainly focus on larger, more popular companies that make millions and millions of dollars every year.

Accounting equation

The accounting equation is simple. Assets equal liabilities plus equity and looks something like this:

Assets = Liabilities + Equity

This equation is a perfect balance. Think of it as a scale. If one side increases, so should the other side to balance it out.

Accounting equation and components

Let's have a look at what each of these components include.

- Assets

An asset is something you own; something you already have. This included things like cash, vehicles, buildings, and patents.

- Liabilities

If something or someone is a liability, it still costs something. This is the amount of money that you might still be owing someone. Liabilities can also be seen as what the creditors will be entitled to if your business were to be liquidated. These liabilities will be paid by your assets which will be taken to cover the amount of money you are owing the creditor. I always advise against buying anything using credit cards or credit lines but in today's day and age, things are too expensive to avoid it completely, not to mention, it is a way of ensuring you have sufficient funds without risking your personal assets all the time. This includes bank loans, personal loans, credit cards, and any other type of loan that you already have but you haven't yet paid for.

- Equity

This is the part of the business that shareholders or partners own. Basically, everything that is left after the liabilities are paid off, goes toward the partners and shareholders. This includes capital, withdrawals, loans, and anything else that the business hasn't paid the shareholders or partners for yet.

Taxes

What are taxes

We all know that taxes are. It's the bane of our existence, hell to the hole, the dagger in the throat.

Okay, that might have been a little dramatic but it got the point across, didn't it?

We all have to pay taxes. It's like going to school or getting a job. It just has to happen. But where you only paid your taxes once a year while you didn't own a business, now you have to pay it four times a year. That's right. Those taxes that you dreaded once a year now could quarterly. There an upside to this, though. Breaking it all up into chunks means that you don't have that huge amount of paperwork to do once a year. Instead, you have to do only small piles four times a year. If you want to open a business, you have to be prepared for the taxes as it's the one thing that you can never avoid.

When you should pay taxes and quarterly taxes

It doesn't matter what size your business is, if you owe income taxes of $1000 or more per quarter, you have to pay the tax. No if's and's or but's. Chances are that you will indeed exceed the minimum amount so taxes are a must. There is also the more complicated part where you have to deposit federal income tax that was withheld from employees and other tedious things on a weekly or monthly schedule. Other taxes included are federal unemployment taxes, social security taxes and Medicare taxes.

Your deadlines for quarterly taxes are:

- April: This covers the period from Jan 1 to March 31.
- June: This covers the period from April 1 to May 31.
- September: This covers the period from June 1 to Aug 31.
- January: This covers the period from Sept 1 to Dec 31.

Calculating these taxes can be tedious and tiresome. It can also get very complicated if you have a lot going on in the business. I would suggest getting a trained professional to do this for you, but if you'd rather do it yourself, I've got you covered.

You have to calculate the following for the year:

- Expected adjusted gross income
- Taxable income
- Deductions
- Tax credits

Once you have done all that, you have to calculate what you'll owe in a year's time and from there you can calculate what you'll have to pay quarterly. The IRS has a very nifty form that will help you estimate your tax. Form 1040-ES is your best friend when you are just starting out. Once you have done your first years' worth of taxes, you can easily calculate the next years' as using it as a template.

Paying the employment taxes is a different story and there is a handful of forms to fill out and deposit along with the money owed. For example, you'll have to fill in Form 941 each quarter for those taxes as well as Form 940. Make sure about the deadline dates for these forms and taxes so you are never late.

Preparing for taxes and what you will need

Being the control freak that I am, I feel the need to stay on top of my taxes from the get go. This means that I keep every single document I need filed and organized perfectly. I also try to calculate my taxes and do my paper word as soon as possible so I don't leave everything for the last possible moment and I have to spend sleepless nights doing them before the deadline is looming over me. Here are some things that need to do your taxes.

- Previous tax return documents if you have already finished a tax return year.
- Payroll documents
- Partnership documents
- Accounting documents
- Bank statements
- Depreciation schedules

Other useful documents to save include gross receipts, sales records, insurance premiums, professional fees, rent, transportation and travel expenses, advertising costs, office supplies and equipment, phones and internet, unclassified income, contractor payments, and employee wages. These documents aren't 1005 necessary but are definitely 100% useful.

Tax deductions

Tax deduction are amazing and if you are not taking advantage of them, you are either stupid or uninformed. Well, now I am informing you, so you have no excuse to let this slide. Don't overpay tax. You are paying enough as it is already. Here are some useful tax deductions that you simply have to take advantage of.

- Company vehicles

There are two ways that you can use your company vehicle to save you some money on for your business. If you can prove that your vehicle is indeed being used for business purposes, you can either go down the standard mileage route or the actual car expenses route. The difference is that standard mileage requires you to keep track of how much you drive the vehicle. This means that you can deduct the cost of operating your vehicle so the math will be the price of gas per mile you drive it. If you decide to go the other route, you will have to keep track of everything that you need to operate your vehicle. This includes gas, repairs, insurance and so on, and so forth. It solely depends on how much the car gets used but you have to work smart. Choose the method that saves you the most money.

- Rent

Your rent is 100% deductible and is a great way to save money. It'll almost be as if you pay double rent if you do not deduct it. Every penny you save is a step in the right direction.

- Insurance

Insurance is a great thing to deduct from your taxes as you can claim 100% of the cost. Every business should have some form of insurance if not a variety of them, so make sure you deduct those costs from the tax. Insurance is not cheap so wherever you can use it to your advantage, do it.

- Inventory

Your inventory is basically materials and supplies, right? So why can't you deduct it? This has been overlooked too many times in the past not to mention. You are able to deduct your inventory costs as well as everything else you sell in the store.

- Startup costs

That is right, my friends. You may have gotten the chills thinking about the money you have to spend on getting the business going as well as paying tax, but the good news is that you can deduct your startup costs as long as it's $50 000 and below. If the amount exceeds that, the amount can be deducted over 180 months. Pretty neat, don't you think?

- Interest on business loan if you have one

Another one that people often overlook and don't think about deducting will be the interest that you have to pay if you have made a loan for the business. This includes the interest on your credit cards, mortgage and business loans!

LEGAL ENTITY EXPLANATION

$\mathcal{O}$n legal matters I believe that it is better to consult with a professional than taking advice from any Tom, Dick, and Harry. There are too many technical things surrounding legal documents and actions that a person who didn't devote years of their life studying it, won't know what is going on, never mind have the ability to help you. As legal matters are so serious, I will advise anyone and everyone to hire their own lawyer and do some research themselves.

I will, however, quickly go over the two main choices for entrepreneurs when it comes to ownership structures.

Sole Proprietorship

The easiest of the two options and probably the most popular, the sole proprietorship option does not split the owner away from their company. This means that you are bound to your company and although it is the easiest way to start a business, you do have a lot of cons that go with it. You will now be vulnerable to lawsuits and other obligations as it is a personal business. Where LLC splits the owner from the business, the sole proprietor is personally responsible for everything concerning the business as they are one and not split up.

LLC

A limited liability company allows a new business to start as its own thing. This means that it is separate and it's its own legal entity. As I have mentioned, describing sole proprietorship, LLC splits the owner from the company. This will protect you against lawsuits and other obligations and keeps the business' finances separate from the owner's. the only exception is the owner's tax. The down part of this is that the paperwork never seems to stop. It is also more expensive than starting a sole proprietorship.

Main differences and benefits

- Taxes

Sole proprietorship's taxes have to be filled on your tax return where an LLC means that you have to fill out separate forms. Which means more paperwork for you. But aside from the paperwork, there aren't really any significant differences between the two where the tax is concerned. One does not have advantages that the other does not and that's the same with the disadvantages. They are both equal on this topic.

- Personal Liabilities

This is where the big differences come in.

A sole proprietor has no protection against lawsuits or anything else as he is personally responsible for the business. This means that the owner's assets are at risk and can be taken by creditors as it is part of the business. A sole proprietor is also much more likely to take out better and bigger business insurances to protect the assets as it is basically everything they own, and they have to protect it.

Putting the paperwork aside, an LLC is the better option in this regard. An LLC ensures that the owner's personal assets are blocked from creditors out for the business' assets. They cannot touch your own assets unless the contract for the money stated otherwise. An LLC creates that little barrier that keeps your assets safe.

There are many other aspects to take into consideration, but I will advise that you see a professional to ensure you make the right decisions. In the end, they both have their pros and their cons, so you have to weigh them up against each other and see which one works best for you and what vision you have for the business. LLC businesses are more likely to be run by a board of partners, whereas a sole proprietor makes all the decisions themselves. However, there is a way around that with LLC and you can structure your LLC company as a single source run company. This will ensure that you are the only person able to make decisions in your company. Although, some LLC companies prefer the team effort of making decisions together and sharing ideas, thoughts and responsibilities. Some companies encourage this above all else.

I think the big question is whether you are a team player or not.

THE PROFIT FORMULA: FOR TRUE FINANCIAL FREEDOM

*T*he goal of your business is ultimately to earn a profit and we often hear stories of people who open their businesses and make a killing from the get go. The problem with these stories is that they are most often false. They like telling people that they have a success rate much higher than they actually have to get clients. The truth is that I have helped a dozen businesses start up, and yes, most of them have been have been successful, but there have been failures. And those success stories? That takes years. Building a business takes years and years of hard work to achieve the main objective. It's not going to happen overnight. There is no way that a business makes a profit that can be considered a 'success' within the first six months, perhaps not even the first year or two. Don't let those stories fool you. If you believe that those things actually happened, then you will feel discouraged when your business isn't as successful as those other fictional businesses.

However, here are a few things you can consider while you are running your shop to increase profit and to help speed up the process.

- Incremental growth

Sure, it's good to think long-term, but what about now? What about the goals you have to reach now? When we are thinking too far into the future, we often miss the opportunities that are presenting themselves to us everyday. Just because they do not lead directly to your end goal, does not mean that those opportunities are any less important to take. Whenever I help a new business, I have the owner sit down and construct a list of things to within the next month. I don't care about your one year or even two year plan. I want to know what your one month plan is. Sometimes it's good to even determine what your one day and one week plans are too. What can you possibly do today or this week that will help you in the future? People often think that you have to work on a long-term plan to help them achieve their goal but those plans hardly ever include the road to the goal. How will you achieve it? This is where you start. You start with small, short plans. You won't be able to do as much as you can in a year, but you are starting somewhere and that is the first step toward success.

- Innovation

Have you seen those Wish adds that pop up on random websites? The ones with the terrible items that you just can't think anyone would buy? All of those products were created with the hope that they would be successful and unique. They were created, hoping that it solves some unknown problems the world might be facing. They are being innovative by creating new products and to be honest, we could learn a thing or two from them. Be innovative with your coffee shop and try new things. Keep things interesting. Try and try until you have found something that is unique, in short-supply, but high demand. Be creative and innovative.

The cellphone is a great example. Telephones were restricted to houses and so the first mobile phone was born in order to solve that problem. Dial up internet service took forever to connect and was slower than a snail. That was when wifi came along. Honestly, without wifi, where would we be right about now? Not everybody could afford physical books. There was no space for it on their bookshelves or they simply didn't like the feel of it. Then some genius thought of e-books and the world went crazy. This is what you want to do with your coffee shop. Perhaps not to that extreme, but it's a good goal to aim for.

- Connections

In today's day and age, you can't get anywhere without the proper connections. But most people don't start off with having a whole bunch of connections, now do they? Your goal is to make some. Speak to everyone and everything. If you are shy, break out of that shell because as a business owner, there is no room for you to be shy. You have to open up your mouth and speak to people. You have to make your own connections. Talk to other businesses in your area, even try making contact with businesses similar to yours. Sometimes they might need your help and in return, they will help you out. Having connections isn't only about knowing people, it's about having something to offer the other person in return for their help. No one does anything for free. Everything is an energy exhange, either in time, money, or trade of skills. That is a lesson I have learned the hard way, and one I hope that you never have to learn yourself. Everyone has an agenda, even you. It's no secret. That agenda you have is what will make a good business great.

- Things that might be holding your business back

Your business has been up and running for months and yet you are still not seeing a difference in profits. Now is the time to sit down and think about the things that might be holding your company back. Think of it like a driving through mud. That is basically what a business is; driving through mud and hoping you don't get stuck anywhere or that you have to ask someone to tow you out. Eventually the mud will stick to your tires and it will make it harder to move the car. It makes the tires slippery and the more you try getting out, the more mud sticks to the tire and the deeper you are sinking into it. What do you do in these situations? You get out of your car and look at the situation from a different angle. You determine where the problem is and then you work on a strategy to fix it. You scrape the mud from the tires with a stick, picking it clean and then you build a solid foundation the tires can grip on to get you out of the hole. If your business is getting nowhere, step outside and have a look at it from another angle. Scrape off the things that are holding you back and build a new foundation, come up with new ideas to get the business out of the hole. It's important to know what is holding you back. You can't fix a flat tire if you don't know that it's flat.

- Drive growth

Your business is an infant and as such, once it stops there is definitely something wrong. It has to grow constantly. Every month, you have to earn more and more money and every year your company has to grow. That is what I define as a successful company.

Much like my previous point, step out of the business for a moment and contemplate your options. Come up with some plans to help your business grow again. It's also important to determine where you want to drive growth. Take the time to think about this every so often.

- Value

Sure, every sale is a profit, but having people return for more is even better.

They way you get customers to return is by adding value to their purchase. When a consumer finds something that they can't get anywhere else, that they actually value such as good, affordable coffee or a fantastic hangout spot with personality like no other. That is the sort of value you want to present to your clients.

Good value also shows that you care and if you care, the customers will care about you as well, even if they don't realize it themselves. It's a certain sort of loyalty that we as humans have. You scratch my back, I'll scratch yours.

I've done a study a while ago where I went to the streets of different locations where I knew that stands (Manhattan, Chicago, and Boston) would be popular and where coffee shops (Newport, Denver, and Port May) would succeed and asked a series of questions. All of them, every single one of them said that value is at the top of their list of needs. The smaller towns enjoyed the idea of having a spot where people could hang out and were welcome to spend the whole day, just hanging out and perhaps even working. When I mentioned a caring and loyal owner, their eyes all but lit up. They want someone who cares. Someone who isn't just in it to take their money. But even if that is your goal, you have to show them that you are not. They will rather support a person who cares about giving the customer the best possible service and products than a place that cuts on costs and serves rubbish.

There was one woman in Manhattan that told me about a food stand guy that she used to buy lunch from. She said that he was the nicest, most caring man she had ever met. His food was great and she got good value for her buck, but she was more excited about seeing him than anyone else. He knew most of his customers by name and would serve them their 'usual' without a second thought. The only reason she doesn't see him anymore is because he fell terribly ill. Most of his customers collected money for his treatment and to keep his business alive until he recovered. People want someone they can make a part of their lives. He was always there, making the best food he can with the resources he could scrape together.

- Customer engagement

This, again, focuses on your target market. You want them to get engaged in your business. The more engagement, the more exposure for you. Exposing your business to more people means more customers which means a higher profit. Get as many people to participate in giveaways as possible and make sure that they involve their friends too. Hold game nights in the coffee shop.

One of the coffee shops I helped was located in Tennessee. It had a cowboy theme and served hearty, old-school cowboy meals. Once a month, the owner hosted a trivia night and the winner won a free meal up to a certain amount for him and his family or friends. New faces appeared every game night and they kept coming back, knowing that there was a chance that they could win something. Those game nights also generated a profit that nearly covered the entire month's rent merely because of the number of people who came and participated. Obviously, they are not going to participate on empty stomachs and dry throats. It's a brilliant way to generate extra profit as well as exposing your business to the world a little more.

- Plan

You cannot go into anything blind. Never when business is concerned. You have to plan ahead and calculate every outcome. Make plans to generate more profits. What can you do to bring more people in? What can you serve the customers that they cannot find anywhere else? It's better to over-plan than not plan at all. It also gives you a general idea of where the company is headed and if you don't like it, you can change the course fast enough. Always keep planning and don't leave any stone unturned. Share plans with the people you trust and ask for help if you need it. There's no shame in it.

- Track it all

I am a complete control freak. I need complete domination of everything in my life. This means that I have a compulsive need to keep track of everything that goes on in my various businesses. This isn't necessarily a bad thing. Where some people might call me a control freak, I like to think of myself as thorough. I hate surprises and everything has to go my way. The only way I can do this is by keeping track of everything and anything in my businesses.

- Profit formula

Probably the most important math you can do in the business is the profit formula. This formula calculates your profit percentage and by doing this, you will know whether or not you should increase or decrease prices. The formula is pretty simple and any person can do it. Trust me, if I can do it, so can you

The formula requires you to subtract your expenses from your sales and then divide that answer by the sales. Here is a simple example

($100,000 sales - $78,000 expenses) ÷ $100,000 sales

= 2.2% profit

There are many other ways that you can calculate this but I have found that this is the most efficient way.

7 MISTAKES MOST PEOPLE MAKE, AND HOW TO AVOID IT

*R*ight, let's take a look at the thing that scares most people away from starting anything; failure. Statistics don't lie. Nine out of 10 businesses fail during the startup phase, which is about the first 3 years. That's right! That means that you have to be one of the 10% if you want your business to be successful. But how do you do that? How can you know that you'll be that 10%? The answer is something that I can't give you. There's no way of knowing how well you will do and whether or not you will succeed. There just isn't a way. What I can tell you, though, is the seven biggest mistakes people make and how to avoid it. This won't guarantee your success, but it will illuminate most of the problems that might kick you out of the 10%. If you memorize what I have taught you, you're already halfway there. The next half consists of you putting that into action and keeping a straight head. Here are some mistakes that people make when starting up their businesses.

- You fall in love

Everybody wants to fall in love, right? Everyone wants to find that beautiful somebody that makes their insignificant life mean something. Some people don't find that in people, though, but instead fall in love with their business. The problem isn't loving your business. You should love it. It's the thing you have been working so hard to achieve. It is all you. All of your ideas, your blood, sweat and tears, your money, and assets. It's all yours and you should love and cherish it. But there's a difference between being in love and loving something. When you love something, you see the flaws, but you love it despite those flaws. When you're in love, you tend to ignore the flaws. You don't see them and refuse to believe that your company has any. No one wants to believe that their partner's voice is annoying. You don't hear it but your friends do.

When I was in high school, I dated a girl that didn't know AC from DC. It was truly terrifying how she got to the grade that she was in. At the time, I thought she was the cutest thing in the world. I was infatuated. I thought that there would never be another girl like her. My friends hated her, though. Whenever I invited them over, they would ask if this girl would be there too and then bailed whenever she was. I could never understand it and there were a lot of fights about it. Then one day, I began to notice the little things. The way she used the wrong words in sentences, the way she confused football with soccer, the way she thought Van Halen was a vampire hunter. That was when I knew that there was a problem and I was losing friends because of it.

The point is that you should keep your eyes open to the flaws in your company. It's not a baby. You're allowed to say that it's ugly and try to fix it. Don't wait until it's too late.

- You either think ahead or not at all

Living in the moment is great and all, but you have to think ahead too. The problem I see often is that people either live in the moment or spend all their time in the future. There has to be a balance. There's a time that you have to think ahead like when you are making big decisions. What impact will that have on your business in the future and how will you handle it then? You have to have a goal that you are working toward and when you are determining what those goals are, you have to think about *how* you are going to get there and *when*. But if you spend too much time thinking about the future and try to solve problems that haven't even risen yet, you are going to miss the small opportunities that present themselves to you in the now. Yes, it's good to work with a plan, but you have to take it one day at a time to make this work. Don't get carried away with the plans for the future either. There is a lot between then and now. But don't block out those plans either because if you don't have a successful future in mind, you will lose interest.

It's easy to get caught up in the bright future and it's even easier to get caught up in the current situation of the company, whether it being bad or good, it happens. The trick is to find the perfect balance between the two.

- Lack of support

As with everything else we do in life, we need a support system that we can rely on. It's easy to fall into a hope and get depressed when no one is supporting you in life and it is one of the biggest flaws I see in people who want to start a business. Now, there are two parts of this.

The first being that you don't need support. Yes, it's nice, but what does that support really do? Does it make you money? Does it pour the coffee? No, it's only a mental thing that people like to use as an excuse. "Oh, my wife doesn't support me." Yes, she's not the one who's doing payroll so don't let it get you down. Blaming it on the lack of support is an easy way out. Be your own biggest supporter.

The second part might sound a little harsh, but it is true nonetheless. You have to earn the support of some people. Perhaps there have been many failed ventures in your past and your spouse is finding it hard to believe that you are going to see this venture through. It's understandable, it really is. You are taking your savings and dedicating your life to this. Of course they'll be skeptical. This is where you have to earn their trust and support. That's right, friends. Get out of that little pity party and prove to people that you can do it with or without their help. You can't rely on other people to do anything for you. You have to do it yourself.

- You don't take the market into consideration

Sometimes people start businesses without taking the market into consideration. They start a vape store while it's going out of fashion, or maybe a bookstore when everything can just be read and ordered online. You can't start a coffee shop if you don't know what the market is like in the area. You are dead-set on doing one thing and you will do it despite the market warning you against it.

If you need investors, will they be willing to invest in your coffee shop? The market will make them decide and if the market says no, then the answer will bea resounding no. You have to be in the right location with the right market. You can't ignore it or your business will fail within months, that I can guarantee it. I have seen it happen before. I have warned people against these things, but no one listens. Be the person who listens to guidance that is provided and consider the market before you start anything. You might have to change locations or themes in order for it to work.

- Can't work with money

One of the businesses I helped start up, one of the few that I don't like mentioning as it failed, had an owner who was clueless about money management. I knew that it was doomed from the start, but I had hoped he would learn a thing or two from me. He never learned.

The problem with him wasn't the business. He had a solid business plan that wowed everyone who read it. He had a good shop in a good location and built up an impressive customer base very early on. On paper, the business looked promising and was a certain success. That was until he got his hands on the money.

There was no cash flow in the business. It was nonexistent. I am still deciding whether he was getting caught up by the cash flow chaos, or if he had poor money management skills. Now, a person who is bad with money usually know that they are. If they got a salary, it would be spent faster than they got it and they are always broke–always. This is the part where you should get a professional to handle the finances because that is not where your talents lie. Taking nothing away from your business management skills or customer service, some people just aren't cut out to work with money and that is why you pay a professional who does it for a living to do it for you.

- You're stiff

Being dedicated to one thing isn't necessarily a bad thing, but you have to keep your mind open to new ideas and be flexible in everything you do with the coffee shop. As the years go on, people change and so do their likes and dislikes. In the 80s, people loved leg warmers and headbands. That trend is long gone and good riddance for that. In 40 years, many of the things that we do and like today will be looked at the same way we are looking at mullets and leopard print tights. Don't close your mind off to new ideas and changes you might have to make to stay relevant in the market. You can't have the same décor for ten years and expect people to find it as charming as they did when you first opened the coffee shop. Do you think that coffee shops 20 years ago thought that pumpkin spice lattes were going to be a thing? Times change and so should you. You need to test the market often to make sure that you are still relevant and if not, it's time to stretch those legs a little and try something new. You don't have to change everything about your business–it's what made it a success in the first place. But try to expand a little. Use what you have and add to that. You have to be flexible to stretch and change with the changing times.

- You want it to be perfect

When something isn't perfect, people lose interest in it. When a child gets a doll and the dog leaves bite marks on the legs, the child will never want to play with the doll again because it's not perfect anymore. That is exactly how it works with adults as well. As soon as you hit the smallest inconvenience, it feels like your life is ending, and you are going to lose everything. One customer complained about the coffee being too strong and now you want to shut down the business because you want it to be flawless.

I have advice for this: Grow up.

We aren't children anymore and there are going to be a lot of bumps in the road. You might even be down to one employee and only have the petty-cash in the company's funds and that is okay because you can get out of it as long as you don't lose all hope entirely. You don't raise a baby because it's perfect. A baby is everything but. They cry, they mess things up, they drive you up the wall sometimes but you never give up on them because they're not perfect. Don't give up on your business either. Most of the time, it will be you who messed up somehow, not the coffee shop, so don't blame it for your mistakes. Toss the idea of perfect out of the window and never look at it again because that word is evil.

Nothing is perfect and the sooner you can accept that, the sooner you can fix the flaws and strive to be as close as perfection as you can. Just know that nothing is ever going to be perfect.

HOW TO SCALE IN YEAR 1

I divided this next part into two because there is a significant difference between scaling in one year and scaling in a longer period of time. There are people that will fight me on this, and I will fight right back. I have gone on and on about being able to think long-term as well as short-term. The reason for it being that there is such a big difference between the two. The scaling that will take place in one year is significantly smaller than the scaling that will happen in say, three years. You cannot combine the two as they are completely different and have different things to keep in mind while doing it.

- Management skills

When you just start out a new business, you are

still a little scared of what to do and how to do things. You are not sure how to manage an entire company, so this first year is basically finding your footing. You have to find the best route to take when making decisions and growing into yourself as a small-business owner. As your company grows, so will your areas that need managing. You will have to employ a manager to help you out as there will come a time that you can't manage anything anymore. It'll become too much. Doing this, management in your company grows. You will also need to develop every management skill that you can in this process because as the company grows, you'll have more and more to oversee, more decisions to make, more plans to execute, more things to manage.

- Collaborate

I will say this again as I have said it before; contacts are important. They always have been and always will be one of the most important things in any area, any business or career. It's just one of those things. As you grow, you will get the opportunity to work with various companies. Some coffee brands might be interested in collaborating with you. Don't turn these opportunities down. They are a great way to grow your business as they will be promoting your coffee shop and in return, you will be promoting their products. Collaborate where you can, but choose your partners wisely. Make sure that they are the sort of company and brand that you want your coffee shop to be associated with.

- Process

With any business, you want workflow to be as simple, efficient and fast as possible. While the business grows into itself as a company, you will begin to figure out what works and what doesn't. You'll realize that the way the coffee is being made takes too long and you'll have to think of a new method that might go faster. Some processes are also more cost-efficient than others so those are definitely worth looking into. There will be a lot of trial and error in this first year of running your business and it's your job to distinguish between trials and errors. Anything that makes the process of making coffee and serving more people is a trial that becomes a victory.

- Core

In a company, there is always the core with a lot of small things surrounding it. Before refining all of those small things, you have to refine the core.

The core of the business is what keeps it running. It's what makes the most money and what has the most value. In the case of a coffee shop, your core is most likely your coffee and serving customers. You have to determine what is the most popular and work on perfecting that.

For example, if you offer the service of sitting down and taking the coffee to go, you have to establish which one makes you the most money. If it's to-go, then you have to speed up the process of making coffee and handing it over to the customer. You have to make sure that your packaging is good so that it doesn't spill and that they are advertising your brand clearly.

If your core values align with people who sit down and have coffee, you have to make sure that they are in a comfortable environment and work on the waiters getting orders and delivering them quickly. Do you see where I'm going with this? Focus on the main income, improve on it, and then move on to the smaller parts of the business.

- Strategies

Once your company is up and running, chances are good that you have already worked on your yearly plan. Where do you see yourself in one year and how are you going to get there? Now comes the part where you have to set those plans into motion. You have to strategize and brainstorm until you have everything worked out and then you have to stick to those strategies and use them to get to your end goal.

- Money, money, money

In this year, you might not make a huge profit, but you are guaranteed to make one. If you see that your company might need a little more money to keep it going, you have to go after investors and get funding. Perhaps take out a loan. The first year is about learning what your business needs and gives you. If it needs more money, give it to it, if it means that you are going to make more money in the long run.

- Stand out

Find your voice and be unique. You want your coffee shop to stand out above the rest. You want it to be special and unique. The first year is where you get to find that uniqueness. It's where you have to decide what you want to be known for as a company and what makes you stand out. Learning the company is a great way to figure that out and once you have found it, you can build on that foundation and milk the uniqueness to draw in more and more customers on a daily basis. Advertise the special bits of your company's personality. The best thing you can do is find a niche and run with it.

HOW SCALE IN YEARS 2-5

*W*here the first year focuses more on building the business, the next couple of years will focus on keeping the business and growing it. The first year is great for getting to know the coffee shop and building a reliable customer base. It's also great for building your team of employees and establishing what you want the business to be and how you want to run it. By the end of the year, you want to have a sturdy foundation to expand and grow on.

In the next couple of years, you are going to grow a lot. There are a lot of things that will change from the start where you actually started the business to where you are going to be in three years. As your business gets older and time progresses, you'll have to look at pricing and advertisements. You have to change with the times if you want to stay relevant.

Here are some things that you can expect in those years.

- Pricing

I used to hate it when my grandfather brought out the old "When I was your age, I could buy a house with the price of a cow today" stories. I hated it. I thought it was the most idiotic thing anyone could say. I always wanted to tell him that his salary was that much less as well but usually knew that keeping my mouth shut was the better option.

But it's a perfect example of how time has an effect on the prices of things. The prices of the things on your menu can't always stay the same. Your rent is going to increase, you'll have to increase salaries, and don't even get me started on the ingredients. Keep a close eye on the pricing of things as time goes on. If the market suddenly plummets and no one is drinking coffee anymore, you might have to adjust your prices accordingly. Never forget about pricing and just leave something as it has been for years. Sure, customers might complain but sooner or later they will realize that everything is getting more expensive.

- Understand the customer

Over the years, you will start to understand

customer behavior and why they do the things that they do. This will allow you to predict what the customer wants and needs at certain stages in life. Why do people come to your coffee shop? Is it mostly sad men and women who are going through things? If it is, you might want to put some comfort food and drinks on that menu of yours.

Customer needs, likes and dislikes will change over the years and you have to stay on top of it.

- Leave a fingerprint

In the end, your main goal should be to leave a mark on the world. I am a firm believer that we should never be forgotten. By leaving a fingerprint, something unique to us and us alone, it is a great way of ensuring that people will always remember us.

You want your company to leave a fingerprint as well not only to be remembered when it's not running anymore one day, but even while it's still alive.

This brings me back to being unique. You have to continuously strive to be unique. Other companies will start copying your style and then what? They say imitation is the purest form of flattery, however strive to maintain your uniqueness. Keep yourself on top of this and make sure that there is always something special about your coffee shop that will attract people's attention.

- Releasing control

Sooner or later, any owner of a business has to step back and release some control. You have worked hard to establish this company and build it from the ground up. You have put your heart and soul into it and now comes the time where you have to throw up your hands and step back. Once a company can run on its own without so much involvement from the owner, that is when you know that you succeeded in building a successful business.

AFTERWORD

In conclusion, as a business owner, I would like to say that there are a lot of troubles and problems that will still cross your path. You will be faced with rivalries and all sorts of lawsuits instigated by the people who you are beating at their own game. But trust me, in the end it will all be worth it. It will be worth seeing happy customers. It will be worth it when you see customers return day after day. It takes a lot of work to start a business and I am not going to tell you otherwise. It takes guts, blood, sweat, and tears, and sometimes, it'll make you want to pull your hair out. You won't succeed if you lay down after the first hurdle. Jump the next one when you come to it and then the next.

A coffee shop is not all about the money, or the accounting or even the coffee. It's about creating a space for people to come together and relax. Once you have that, I can guarantee that you will have a loyal customer base that will stick by you through thick and thin. If you have a coffee stand, there will be people who are excited to get to work only to get your coffee. Remember that when you are feeling like you can't run this business.

This book made to help yours do the same. It is my sole purpose to add your name to the people I have helped in the past.

REFERENCES

Gregory, S. (2019). 11 Simple Steps for a Successful Brand Building Process | FreshSparks. Retrieved from https://freshsparks.com/successful-brand-building-process/

Low, A. (2017). The Average Rent for Retail Space. Retrieved 24 October 2019, from https://bizfluent.com/info-8729672-average-rent-retail-space.html

Merrill, T. How to Find Real Estate Deals: Tips & Best Practices | FortuneBuilders. Retrieved from https://www.fortunebuilders.com/how-to-find-real-estate-deals/

Spaeder, K. (2004). How to Find the Best Location. Entrepreneur. Retrieved from https://www.entrepreneur.com/article/73784

Made in the USA
Columbia, SC
16 February 2021

33036883R00090